National Writers Series

Traverse City
2024 LITERARY JOURNAL

National Writers Series
Traverse City

Cover Art: Magoon Creek Beach by Jonas Carlson

Cover Design: Andrea Reider, Designer for Mission Point Press

Editor: Ari Mokdad, Education Director for National Writers Series

2024 Cover Artist Bio:
The middle son of three boys, Jonas Carlson is in seventh grade at Manistee Middle High School. He plays trombone in band and enjoys urban exploring. He has an interest in buildings and landscape photography.

National Writer Series

2024 Literary Journal

National Writers Series
Traverse City

CONTENTS

Manistee Raising Writers

2024 Winter Antrim Raising Writers

2024 Winter Manistee Raising Writers

2024 Winter Writers Create!

Writers Studio

2024 Literary Short Story

2024 NWS Scholarship Winners and Highly Commended Works

Fiction

Journalism

Poetry

Nonfiction

Introduction

The National Writers Series (NWS) is a year-round book festival held in Traverse City, MI. Although we are well-known for hosting world-class and best-selling authors from around the globe, our mission is to support young writers by offering free creative writing classes to our region.

Each year, NWS showcases the work of our Raising Writers programs. This year, we expanded our reach to the Manistee and Antrim communities, and we are proud to feature these wonderful middle school and high school students in the *National Writers Series Traverse City 2024 Literary Journal*. This year, we have also included students from the Writers Studio at the Northwest Ed Career Tech. It is with great pleasure that we have assembled this journal and we celebrate the students' commitment to the literary arts.

You'll find stories, essays, poems, plays, and excerpts from novels written by students throughout their courses and semester-long studies. NWS has been honored to work alongside some of our region's best creative writing teachers who have devoted their time, energy, and compassion in mentoring students towards their creative dreams.

NWS is dedicated to building the skills of our future storytellers, poets, playwrights, and more. One day, we hope to invite an alumnus from our program as the featured author of our author events!

We are looking forward to continuing our educational offerings and are grateful to the countless individuals who have helped make this journal possible. These free creative writing classes would not be possible without the support and dedication of our community. If you are interested in supporting our programs, please contact NWS Executive Director Anne Stanton at director@nwstc.org. You can find more information about our classes, scholarships, and more at nationalwritersseries.org.

–Ari Mokdad, Education Director for NWS

The Art of the Story

Fall 2023 Class

INSTRUCTOR INTRODUCTION: THE ART OF THE STORY FOR MIDDLE SCHOOLERS

Karin Killian

"What is a story? And why do we human beings tell them to each other?"

I asked this dynamic group of middle schoolers these two questions at the beginning of our first class, in the gorgeous room overlooking the Boardman River in the Common Grounds building last September. The students' responses were as varied as their personalities, but all followed the same theme: *we tell stories to connect with one another.* Whether we are looking for entertainment or escape, the stories we tell, and read, and listen to and watch on screens, help us understand each other.

Over the eight weeks that followed, these amazing students learned about the basic building blocks of stories, and then dove right into writing their own. Some of the stories in this collection were inspired by stories we read in class, like "The Wife's Story" by Ursula K. LeGuin, and "Sticks" by George Saunders, yet each student made the prompts their own.

One thing I love seeing in young writers is their love for fan fiction! This is a great way for young writers to learn the tricks of storytelling. That is, by paying close attention to how their favorite TV shows are written, and writing their own in response. Parents can ask questions ask their writers about about the structures of TV episodes and movies, and how their writers chose to tell those stories, and story, and why we think they decided to do it that way, and even, maybe, how a story would be different if told from a different point of view, if they would like to continue this education at home!

This group of kids had such wonderful energy, vivid imaginations and prolific pens! I believe that a couple decades from now, there will be a lot of book jacket bios that say—grew up in Traverse City, Michigan, because these kids have so many more stories to tell.

Keep writing, my friends. *I cannot wait to read more of your stories!*

ADVENTURES WITH BLUEY
Ryleigh Brunson, fifth grade

One day, it was a babysitting day for the Hellers. That meant Uncle Radley was coming over and Aunt Frisky was coming too.

DINGDONG! The doorbell rang.

The door was a bright brown with a plush bird by it.

"Uncle Rad!" Bingo yelled as she went to the door.

Bingo was a bright, orange red heeler with a cream color by her jaw connecting to her forehead.

"Bluey!" Rad said as he scooped up Bingo.

Uncle Rad was a mixed blue-red heeler. With a nice hair style. "I'm Bingo!" she said, "Oh, sorry...Bingo?"

Rad still didn't get it. "Uncle Rad!" Bluey ran.

Bluey was a blue heeler with light blue fur and yellow fur around her jaw and dark blue fur by her eyes.

"Bingo!" Rad said as he scooped her up too.

"Aw come on," Bingo yelled.

"Sup, Rad!" Bandit said. Bandit was Rad's younger brother, he had light blue fur with a big black fur covering his two eyes.

"Sup bro." Rad said as he gave bandit a handshake.

"Are you keeping them for today?" Bandit said as he pointed at Bluey and Bingo. "Yep," Rad said. "See you later."

"Bye girls!" Bandit said as he went to his bright red jeep.

"Bye dad!" Bluey and Bingo said. "All right girls, I need you to do something for me quick!," Rad said quickly. "I need you girls to write a love letter, while I get some flowers from your garden." Then Rad ran to the back yard to get some flowers.

"For who?" Bluey asked.

"For Frisky." He spoke.

Bluey and Bingo looked at each other for a second and did a "Eeeeeee!!!!", so they went to their room to start writing.

Their room was a bright pink with lights across. It had two beds with one lowercase b and a capital B.

"Okay Bingo what about you tell me what to write and I can—" Bluey was not done speaking, until Bingo interrupted.

"What about a heart?" She said.

"Like a drawing of a heart that at the bottom it said love Rad huh?" Bingo finished.

"Yeah!" Bluey yelled. So then for a while, Bluey was drawing the heart while Bingo looked for Frisky.

"Finished!" Bluey yelled.

"Aw cool!" So then at the right time Aunt Frisky was here. She had cream color fur and had wavy hair. Bluey and Bingo ran out to give her the letter.

"Hi Aunt Frisky!" they said.

"Hi girls!" she said.

"Uncle Rad wanted us to give you this."

Bluey gave Frisky the letter and ran inside. Then Rad ran out with the flowers and saw Frisky reading the letter. Then she gave him a smile and went to give a hug.

"We are going to have a new cousin, are we?" Bingo asked.

"Yes, we are." Bluey said.

THE END.

A WRITER'S RAINBOW
Addison McGurn, seventh grade

The walls in the room were painted white. White. White as a blank page, ready to be written on. A blank page makes me feel free. Alive. Like I can do anything. Like I can breathe.

Our teacher had green boots on. Dark green boots with wooden heels that clomped against the carpeted floor as she walked. I wondered if she was planning lessons to come as she made her way across the room. Or maybe she was a super villain and was plotting evil schemes for that night.

I looked down at my feet, noticing the geometric shapes splattered across the rug. There were red squares, blue triangles, and yellow pentagons placed against a (somewhat dirty) dark tan background. The girl sitting across from me had shoulder-length golden curls. I watched as she tucked them behind her ear revealing bright pink tips.

The boy on the left side of her had a silver laptop, with an old yoda sticker on the back. They looked sad; Yoda and the boy both. The plastic-y cover on the sticker had started to rub off, making it so half of yoda's wrinkly light green face underneath was already gone.

The girl on the right side of the girl with curls, the one with an orange cat ear headband, looked pleased with her writing. Excited, even. I looked at her for a bit, wondering, thinking. I didn't know what she was writing, but the longer I watched her, the more eager I grew to find out. She looked up at me, realizing I was staring at her. It was fascinating. She acted as though she was waking up from a deep sleep; a slumber filled to the brim with imagination and dreams. She smiled at me, and I smiled back. Sounds of people typing, and of pens scritching against paper filtered in through one of my ears, and out the other, as I worked on my own writing. I guess I was just so used to it now, that I didn't hear noise at all, which was weird to think about.

I was sitting in a black chair. A surprisingly comfortable black chair. I looked around at all of my classmates. Fellow artists. Fellow creatures. Fellow writers.

Some were writing in notebooks, some were typing on computers. Most -if not all- of them were creating; imaging words that didn't yet exist anywhere else but inside their heads.

Boots clomping against the floor once again, shook me to life. Our teacher looked around the room; eyes brightening. She was clearly delighted with the idea of all of us; young writers from the ages of ten to thirteen, all sitting at a table together. To be honest, I was happy too. She took a deep breath, calming herself before starting class. "All right," she said, projecting her voice around the room. "Let's begin.

DRIFTING
Ellie Florip, fifth grade

I turned over to look at my clock, listening to the seconds ticking by. "Nine thirty two already?" I mumbled as I rolled over, trying to figure out if I should still meet Mia at the beach.

I didn't want to go to the beach but I also didn't want to disappoint her. Three years ago, my sister, Gwen, almost drowned. And ever since, our parents never let us go near the water, they didn't even teach them how to swim.

I sighed. I couldn't let Mia down, she was probably already heading to the beach. It's too late to back out anyway, we were meeting there at nine forty five.

I slowly got up, making sure I didn't make a sound as I slipped two fluffy pillows under the covers. I stepped back to admire my work. I couldn't see very well with only the dim night light on my dresser, but I couldn't risk anybody noticing brite light seeping under my door in the middle of the night.

I slowly closed my door and froze when it groaned. A few seconds later I crept forward and slowed as I neared Gwen's room. When I pressed my ear against the door I was greeted by her loud snoring. Even at night Gwen was the loudest person on earth.

I was halfway down the stairs when I heard a door upstairs open. Soon after, I heard Gwen yawn and flinched as the floorboards creaked above me. I held my breath, waiting for her to catch me sneaking out. Relief flooded over me when I heard her shut the door and her loud snores returned. I had never been so glad to hear Gwen's snores in my entire life.

I quietly ran down the rest of the stairs and slid out the door, shutting it lightly behind me. At least this door is quiet, I thought.

I sucked in the warm summer air as I walked along the sidewalk leading to the beach. I clutched my teal pendant that hung around my neck on its small gold chain, hoping my parents wouldn't catch me.

As soon as Mia saw me she ran towards me with her arms outstretched and her long red hair flowing behind her. I caught a glimpse of her bright green eyes before she embraced me.

"Lizzy! You're finally here!" Mia exclaimed as she let go of me.

"I can't be that late," I smiled at my best friend as we walked towards the water. Mia was the only person besides my family who knew I couldn't swim.

When we were a few feet away from the water I sat down and Mia plopped herself next to me. I stared at the glittering sea in front of, watching as the last rays of sun disappeared beyond the horizon.

"Can we go in?" I asked, my voice shaking. I was scared but I didn't want to be afraid of something that was all around me.

Mia looked surprised. "You sure?" she asked.

I nodded, not trusting my voice as I got up and walked steadily to where the waves crashed on the shore. I could see my short golden blonde hair and caramel brown eyes in the water and next to it I saw long red hair and green eyes.

I dipped one foot in and shivered as I made contact with the water. I took a few more steps in and jumped when something brushed up against my foot.

Mia laughed as I ran away from where I was standing. "It's just a fish, calm down."

I laughed with her and I accidentally splashed water on her which just made me laugh harder.

"Hey!" I exclaimed as Mia splashed water in her face. We kept splashing each other back and forth until we both got tired and I realized we were already neck deep in water.

It was too late, my feet slipped from underneath me and I could no longer feel the sand between my toes. "Help!" I screamed.

Out of the corner of my eye I caught a glimpse of Mia swimming towards me with a giant pineapple floatie.

"Get on," Mia ordered as she got close enough for me to grab on. I struggled to get on, the waves kept crashing over my head, my muscles were screaming and my throat and nose burned from the salty water. Once I was on, I coughed up lots of water and Mia asked, "Lizzy, are you okay?"

"I think so." I replied, shivering when I realized I could barely see the shore, we were at least a mile away from the beach.

Just when I was starting to think I would never see my family again, a stick drifted by and I snatched it from the water with so much force it sprayed water all over us. We might actually see our families again, if we could figure out which way to go.

"How are we supposed to know which way to go?" I asked, annoyed that we weren't better prepared for the situation.

Mia tapped her sparkly bracelet for a few seconds as she stared into the ocean and stopped to reply, "I'm not..." she trailed off and her face lit up. "Wait, doesn't the sun rise right behind your house?"

I nodded as I realized what she was saying. I turned around to search the sky, stopping when I spotted bits of pink blossoming in the sky. I grabbed the stick and used it like a paddle to steer us towards the rising sun as the first bits of sunlight pierced the dark sky.

THE GIRL'S STORY
Emma Grace Schulert, fifth grade

The love-letters started on (I think) April 5th, 2023. I don't know why they're here. If I did, this wouldn't have become an "extreme situation." In fact, maybe I would've enjoyed reading them. After all, I do like these types of things. But this is serious. A life threat, even. And it ruined my entire life.

A long time ago, me and my best friend Lauren were talking about how terrible lunch was as we were walking down the hallway at East Middle School. "Eww! That's *so* gross! Right?" Lauren giggled as we approached my locker. "Yuck! Definitely! Are they trying to poison us or something?" We both laughed hysterically. I think that Lauren and I have been best friends since kindergarten, and maybe we have a tight relationship. I'm not sure though, my mind is a bit foggy today. My thoughts were interrupted by what I saw. I gasped as I saw what was sticking out of my locker. Sitting right there, was a bubble gum-pink letter with *my name on it!* My heart started thumping like a rabbit's foot.

"What's that, Mary?" Swooned Lauren. "A love letter, perhaps?" She snatched it from my locker's grasp. Lauren gasped. "It's anonymous! Who do you think it's from?" I suddenly felt a pang of some sort, as if I knew the answer. Yet, I didn't know a thing about this so-called "love-letter."

"I-I don't know. Well, let me read it at least." I said timidly. So, I took the note right out of Lauren's hands and read.

Dear Mary,
Your eyes sparkle like a sunset and shimmer like a star. They glow in the night but not from afar. Yes, you are so close to me that I feel like I have known you all my life. And yet I have just decided now that I want you to be my wife.

Yours Truly,

ANONYMOUS

I didn't understand. It made no sense at all. I've now read this twice... it just makes no sense at all. I don't remember reading this the first time. All I know is that I've read this before.

After school, I tried my best to remember my way home. Luckily, I carry a map around. Or do I? I don't remember. I tried to shake my thoughts off, but this is crazy.

Three hours later, I finally got home.

"Mary! Why didn't you take the bus like I told you to?! You know I worry about you." My mother cried.

"I was supposed to take the bus?" I asked.

I didn't think I was supposed to take the bus. Although, I had no memory of this morning either.

"Oh, Mary. I'm so sorry. I forgot about- never mind, it doesn't matter. Go wash up, dinners on the table. We're having Fettuccine Alfredo. I'll wait for you." As I headed upstairs, I wondered what she was talking about. What was she about to say? What was she sorry about? Maybe I didn't want to know. So, I tried to not care.

Wait- hold on, what did Mom say to do? I didn't remember. So, I went into my room and did _something,_ but I don't remember what that was.

The next couple of days were all a blur, but the one thing I _do_ remember (they're kind of hard to forget) were those mysterious love-letters. But the strange thing was the fact that they started to get, well, kind of mean & threatening. The first three letters were kind of nice, though they were all the same.

Mary-
Even though you're nice and cool, you do in fact tend to drool. I guess
your hair is somewhat smooth, but it looks like a rat's nest when you
jump, dance, & move.
So, all in all, I think you're nice, but maybe you should talk a little
louder (because your voice sounds just like a group of mice).
I don't really care-
-anonymous

I know- super weird. The next note was extremely scary, though...

MARY!!!
YOU SILLY OLD FOOL! CAN'T YOU TAKE A CLUE? I AM
ALWAYS HERE! I'M ALWAYS WITH YOU! I SEE YOU OVER
HERE, I SEE YOU OVER THERE TOO! JUST REMEMBER
ME PLEASE!

-YOU KNOW ME MARY J. KEYS!!!

Throughout the week, I tried my best to think of who wrote those notes. Justin? Robert? George? I didn't think so. That handwriting was far too neat for them. Hmm... now that I think about it, it sort of looks familiar. Kind of like- no, it couldn't be.

I really needed professional help! Sadly, I didn't have that kind of money for a detective or something. So, the only thing I could do now is to go to the counselor—Ms. Amanda Larkin, the lady with the weirdest accent I couldn't make out.

"WHEY HEH-LLO, MAH-REE! HOW AH-RE YAH TOH-DAY?! GEED, I PRAH-ZOOM (Why hello, Mary! How are you today? Good, I presume)!" Boomed Ms. Larkin.

Geeze, she's so loud that I bet the aliens on Mars could hear her!

"Um, good, but I really have to talk to you about-"

"WHOOT HAHNEY? WHOOT DU YAH HAH-VE TYUE ZAY, MAH-REE (What honey? What do you have to say Mary)?!"

Man, I could barely get a word out with her blabber-mouth!

"Well, I've been getting these, 'ahem', love-letters. And, I have no idea who wrote them. But wait! There's more. So, all of these letters seem so familiar! I feel as if I've read them all a second time, but I haven't! It's so weird! I even recognize the handwriting..."

She looked very surprised. "WOOL MAH-REE, LAHT MAY ZAY DESE LAHV-LUZZERS! DAHD YAH BROONG DEM? I HYUPE

YEH DOHD (Well Mary, let me see these love-letters! Did you bring them? I hope you did)!"

Well, in fact I did, so I handed them to Ms. Larkin. It took a long time, but after she wrote some things down on her clipboard, she told me something I've been waiting to hear my whole life. This time, she softened her voice more than I've ever seen her do before. "Mah-ree, dyue yah rah-lay wahnt tyue knoo dah ansah (Mary, do you really want to know the answer)?"

Yes! Yes! A million times yes!

"I-I think so..." I quietly said.

"Ah-keigh Mah-ree, dizz mooght bah hored fah yah tyue undahstuned, baht yue hahve Ahmeneesua, whach muenns yue hahve ah raileu bahd maymohreigh priblome. Doo yah unertahned (Okay Mary, this might be hard for you to understand, but you have Amnesia, which means you have a really bad memory problem. Do you understand)?" Wait- I do? Well, that explains a lot! But what does that have to do with anything? "Well, I understand but why does that matter in this situation?" She stared at me hard. "Wrute meigh ah nohmce pahem, playse (Write me a nice poem, please)."

I did so, and it looked like this-

You're as kind as a puppy and as sweet as a bird.
Everyone loves you, and you're always heard.
Helpful, lively, well mannered too.
I hope you really like me, because I like you too.

-M. J. K

"Jhost ahse Iye suezpahctued. Mah-ree, yah ahre dah une hyue hahze bune wraghtung deeze luuhtaze. Ahned dah wahst deighn ize daught dyue wught rimonbah diz evah hahpeighned (Just as I suspected. Mary, <u>you</u> are the one who has been writing these letters. And the worst thing is that you won't remember this ever happened)."

All I could hear was the sound of my heart thumping. And thumping. And thumping. "What if this would go on for the rest of my life? I would always forget everything and anything. And I would keep receiving these horrible, nasty letters for the rest of my life! And I would never, ever remember that *I* was the one who was writing them! Maybe this had already happened before! And I would never know. I have now missed out on my entire life!

I ran as fast as I could out of the school and into the parking lot with the cold, cold, rain. I slipped and fell onto the ground. Crying was the only option now.

But wait- what if this is a good thing?

"HAHAHAHA! I'LL SHOP LIFT, STEAL, AND DO ANYTHING I PLEASE! AND I'LL NEVER REMEMBER ALL THOSE THINGS THAT I'LL DO! HAHAHAHAHA! OH, WHAT FUN I'LL HAVE!" I cried.

And then, for the rest of my life, I did all of those horrible things. Again, and again, and again...

"Mary! Time to take your medicine!"

NEVER ENDING FIRES
Sadie Snyder, sixth grade

I stared down at my worn bare feet. They were streaked with dirt, and thin cuts ran along my poor toes. Purple bruises stood out on my pale skin and a beam of sun shone on them, before it disappeared under a dark looming cloud. My feet floated in the crisp water of the river. It was fiercely chilly and it felt like icy needles jabbing into my feet. You would think it was uncomfortable (and you are correct), but the dark water of the river seemed to clean a portion of the dirt off. I was sitting on a log that was beached on the side of the river. Its musty brown bark was rough and scraped my hand when I rubbed it anxiously.

The forest that sat to the east looked dark and gloomy. Strangely, the river didn't shine in the sun as usual, either. People sat all around us, murmuring quietly. Some sat on blankets or towels. Others just lay on the dewy grass and mud on the banks of the river.

My best friend Haylee sat next to me on the log. I could tell that she was quietly pondering to herself, from the look on her face. I turned away, listening carefully to the sounds around me. I could hear a couple of men and women speaking softly nearby. They were gossiping about how our small town didn't stand a chance. I tried not to stare, but they noticed me and attempted to put on brave faces. Even I could tell they were worried, and I'm not great at reading emotions.

Maybe that's why it took me two years to make a friend. Haylee.

We had both lived here our whole lives and we liked lots of the same things. An image of my mom popped into my mind. She would have known what to do. How to make everyone happy again. Suddenly the wind started to pick up, and seemed to blow my thoughts away. Back to reality. I turned toward Haylee and noticed her shoulder-length blond hair dancing in the air. The river started to get wavy. It gently lapped my toes as Haylee scooted closer to me on the log.

Her soft blue eyes were suddenly fierce as she gazed at all the people that were just sitting there, hoping and praying that their hard earned homes would stay standing. The river current was getting stronger, and chilly blasts of ice water sprayed my face. I spluttered and scooted back a bit on the log. I had hoped that would make Haylee smile, but it didn't.

I had never seen her go without smiling for this long.

"Do you think...?" She asked, fixing her eyes on me.

"Nah, I bet that it was just a false alarm." I said cautiously, eyeing a small child that started to cry in his mothers lap. His eyes glazed over with wet tears. A single drop fell down his face and left a shiny trail that a stray beam of sunlight highlighted, before it was covered with a cloud. His mother gently wiped it away and started to cradle him lovingly.

I missed my mom.

What would she have done? What would she possibly have said to make this better?

"Don't worry about it Haylee." I told her uncertainty, "That man was a crazy old lunatic."

Haylee's eyes darkened. She turned away and sighed uncomfortably. "Maybe. But he was a crazy old lunatic who had the entire army with him and a bomb alert."

A cloud rolled over the sun and a droplet of bitter cold rain stung my arm. My neck hair seemed to stand on its ends. A streak of lightning danced in the sky and thunder rumbled in the distance. The baby wailed louder. His mother tried to hush him, but he seemed intent on distracting everyone from the fact that our town may be blown to smithereens. Sadly, it only made the clench in my already double knotted stomach worse.

The crying reminded me of my dad. When I was young, my dad would rock me to sleep. He would hug and rock me when I was fussy and prepare me dinner every night. For some kids, that's the mother's job. But my mom was always busy. She always had something to type or forms to fill out.

She was a firefighter. I always looked up to her. When she was home, she was so brave and strong. She could make the saddest, most unhappy person sing with joy.

But one day, she never came home. All I remember is a man I didn't know wearing all black and white coming to our house that night. It was after my bed time and normally my dad would have swooped me up and swung me around, bringing me back to my bed for the second time. But this time, he just turned around and opened his arms. I ran into them and that was when I knew.

My mom was not coming back. I would never see her again. The baby continued to scream by the river and Haylee avoided my eyes.

Another blast of frigid water splashed me and I pursed my lips. My mom had stopped fires.

Hundreds of them. She never cared how dangerous the job was. But would she be able to stop a bomb? Possible war? Would she care how dangerous that was?

I hugged my knees and waited.

THE JOURNEY
Ziva Erlenbeck, fifth grade

Lark after lark came and went, always coming, always going. Generation after generation. They had always lived in that forest, with the view of a stretch of water that seemed endless. Lake Michigan. Every sunrise every sunset shown radiantly across the water.

Then one day a strange gray cloud rose up from the trees, the creatures of the forest had never seen it before but through some secret knowledge passed down by previous generations they knew what it was, *Fire*. The fire tore through the forest like a vicious beast destroying everything in its path as it glittered deadly beautiful shades of crimsons, reds, and oranges more ferocious than a dying sun. They fled toward the water, their instincts blazing. As they neared the water they began to doubt but they knew there was no other option.

They flew and flew across the gently glimmering turquoise blue waters east toward the horizon. They continued to fly, growing more and more tired. Finally, at last land was in sight, growing larger and larger as they neared the unfamiliar shore. A strange place with great hills of sand with the waves gently lapping the beach like a mother cat as they examined the sandy barren land. They searched around for food but it was scarce so they traveled further inland. Then they found the perfect place, a forest glittering lush emerald green in the golden dappled sunlight not too far from the shore, just in case another fire swept through.

Then again time passed and larks came and went, generation after generation. Overlooking the great waters that had brought them there. "Lake Michigan".

THE BIRD
Madeline Gartland, eighth grade

Everyday I woke up to the sound of Ronnie singing a duet with her bird. We were five when Ronnie and I found the tiny yellow and gold parakeet trembling under a red and gold leafed tree. Ronnie, who had no fear at the time, scooped up the little bird and brought it home. Our mother, with a sigh, begrudgingly agreed to let Ronnie keep it as long as she properly took care of it. Ronnie and her new bird, Melon, were inseparable. One could not be seen without the other.

The years went by. I left home and moved on to start my own life. Ronnie became an artist and continued living with our mother. Before I could register what was going on our mother passed away. Ronnie was devastated beyond repair. She stopped talking, stopped painting, stopped being Ronnie. I went home to help her get through that rough time. When I got there I found Melon bringing paint and paintbrushes to Ronnie. It was as if Melon knew that Ronnie needed help getting back on her feet. I stood for hours and watched as Melon brought Ronnie all her favorite things. I watched as Ronnie picked them each up and stared at them all for a long while. When Melon was done she settled into Ronnie's lap. A teardrop fell silently down Ronnie's face. She was back.

Many decades later I came home for the last time, well into my late 80s. Where I found Ronnie finally at peace, leaning against her art easel. Melon was resting on her shoulder, singing a soft and sad tune. I picked up Melon and brought her to the window, where I released her into the autumn leaves. Her golden wings glistening in the sun as she flew off into the waterfall of red and gold leaves.

THE MIDNIGHT INVASION
Madison Jancek, sixth grade

When I awoke the room was pitch black. I felt around until I could feel for my sword, and slowly tried to stand up, but my knees buckled and I fell to the floor. I slowly crawled over to the wall and used that for support. This time, I stayed standing, but I was overcome with an overwhelming sense of nausea, that I felt like I was going to pass out again. I closed my eyes until I centered myself, and when I did, I stumbled over to the window to open the curtains. However, this provided very little light because it was Midnight. I reached my hand out to the wall so I could keep my balance while I walked over to the door. When I opened it, I saw the familiar hallway I had seen since my childhood. The Navy walls complemented by the polished wood floors. On the left, there were two doors. One led to my parent's room and the other led to my brother's old room. My heart ached when I thought of my brother. Our country is at war and my brother was the captain of the guard. One night, he was assassinated by an enemy soldier and he never even got a burial.

After I swallowed my emotions, I turned right in order to find my perpetrator. I kept walking and entered the family library, a large room with dark bookshelves that went floor to ceiling. I heard footsteps, so I dove behind the elegant leather couch, and held my breath. A large middle aged man, who was balding entered the room. He was at least six feet tall and easily towered over me. He also carried a battle ax. My heart raced as I thought of my next move. When he turned his back, I leapt out from behind the couch and hit him in the back of the knees with the blunt side of my sword. I turned to face him and extended my sword under his chin.

"Drop your weapons or your head rolls." I said. I was bluffing and had no real intention of harming him. He dropped the battle ax and the sword that was sheathed at his side.

"All of them." He grunted, but added a pocket knife. I kicked the items to the side and asked, "What is your purpose of coming here?"

"Why should I tell you?"

"Because I'm the one holding the sword here. Now, let me ask again. What is your purpose of coming here?"

"I was sent by King Allistar of Izallya to assassinate you." This deeply puzzled me. I wasn't of any importance. Unless... No. It couldn't be. My parents were dead.

Two weeks earlier, my father had convinced my mother to go on a voyage to Izallya to sign the peace treaty that would end our three-year long war. The only reason someone would want to kill me was if they had died. That would mean I would have the right to the throne. I was in utter shock until I realized my prisoner was trying to reach his weapons. I leapt in front of him and again put my sword under his chin.

"I won't harm you if you give me answers. What is your name?" I asked.

"Karvin."

"And what do you know about my parent's deaths?"

"I only know that they died at sea, before they ever reached land."

I lowered my sword. "You are free to go as long as you do two things. First, never return here unless you have a death wish. Two, Tell King Allistar that if I find out that he was connected to their deaths, that I would continue this war until every last Izallian bowed before me, including him." He nodded, quickly gathered his things, and exited down the stairs, and through the front gates of the castle. When I was sure he had left, I slumped against the nearest wall. I let all my emotions pour out at once. I sat there for what must've been hours because it was now dawn, and sun rays gently gleamed through the window. Once I finally had the strength to stand, I roamed around my castle, feeling more alone than ever, contemplating what I should do. These next few months would be devastating. Our armies were tired from the on-going war, and our supplies were dwindling. I was going to have to make some difficult decisions that could end up in the deaths of my people, and I wasn't totally sure I could.

Jonas Carlson

Summer 2023
Writing Fantastic Stories

INSTRUCTOR INTRODUCTION: SUMMER 2023 WRITING FANTASTIC STORIES

Kevin Fitton

The Writing Fantastic Stories Workshop took place during July 2023 as a part of the Northwest Michigan College's College4Kids program. Eight students between fifth and eighth grade took part in the class and threw themselves headlong into their work.

The heart of the class was learning about the types of fantasy stories, and then using those story-types as a model for developing our own fantastic story. Scholars have identified four types of fantasy stories: 1) The portal-quest story, where a character leaves the "real" world and enters a magical world (i.e. *The Lion, the Witch, and the Wardrobe*), 2) The intrusion story, where a world of magic intrudes upon the "real" world (i.e. *Harry Potter* or *Dracula*), 3) The immersive story, that takes place in an entirely different world (i.e. *The Lord of the Rings*), and 4) The liminal story, in which it is never fully clear whether the world of the story is magic or not (i.e. *The Headless Horseman* or *Coraline*).

Each of these types of fantasy story has its own purpose, and we discussed those narrative purposes as we worked on writing our own stories. Students generated a number of ideas through exercises and free writing. Then they picked a favorite idea and worked on that story for the rest of our week together. As the instructor, I was surprised when I came up with an idea for a story where playing a certain piano a certain way transported my character into a different world. It's an idea I plan to keep working on (maybe it will be a children's book).

THE GIFT
Ava Montero, seventh grade

"Be on you best behavior. Okay, you two?" Mom said, glancing at me and my twin sister in the rearview mirror.

"We always are," my sister Amina said, winking at me.

I smiled, "Mom, how can you doubt us?

"Because I know my daughters. Now, no funny business."

"Your Mother's right, girls," Dad said from the passenger's seat.

"Okay," we both said.

We were on the way to the reading of our Great-Great Aunt Celia's will. My mom was giving us the usual "no funny business" talk because Amina and I were famous for our pranks.

"And please," Mom continued, "be polite. If Aunt Celia left us any-thing, be humble, and remember that she passed away, okay?"

"Of course," Amina said, smiling at me with twinkling eyes.

"Do you remember when Aunt Celia would play that game with us where her house was magic?" I asked.

"Yes! And every time we came to her house she would tell us a story about her adventures with one magical thing or another!" Amina exclaimed.

"All right girls, we're here," Mom said, pulling into the parking lot of the lawyer's office.

We met up with all of our family and greeted them in the parking lot.

Uncle Joe led the way towards the big building. All thirty-two of us crowded inside the lawyer's small office, which held two chairs available for us to sit on.

"Oh!" said the lawyer, a tall, balding man in a gray suit, "I didn't know there would be so many of you." He pushed up his glasses.

"Yes. Well, we're here," Uncle Joe said, giving him a stiff smile.

"Yes, I can see that," the lawyer said, stretching out his hand across his desk for Uncle Joe to shake. "I'm Will Evans, the attorney who handled Celia Andrew's Estate." He made his way around, shaking the hands of all the adults. He again pushed up his glasses and cleared his throat.

"Shall we get started?" he asked as he walked over to his desk and picked up a folder. Opening it, he lifted out a crisp paper and pushed up his glasses yet again.

"A-hem," he began. "I, Celia Andrews, state that this is my last will and testament. I bequeath all of my jewelry, makeup, and clothes to my two daughters, Analise and Gloria." Aunt Celia left all of the adults and kids money. She left to her son the house and all belongings, except for the items she gave to certain family and friends who had sentimental connections to them.

"And last but not least," Will Evans read, "I leave the locked chest in the closet in my bedroom to my great-great nieces, Amina and Alexa. You will find the key sitting in the white porcelain dish on my dresser. Open the chest when you are at home, in one of your rooms. I love you all very much and wish that you will celebrate my life instead of mourning my death. I will see all of you again one day, but until then, I wish you all lives filled with laughter, love, hope, faith, and joy."

Will Evans set down the paper and looked around the room. Everyone was murmuring and whispering to one another.

I looked at Amina in confusion. "I don't understand. Why would Aunt Celia leave us a locked box sitting in her closet? I don't remember ever seeing that. Do you?" I asked.

Amina shook her head. "I'm confused, too. Maybe we'll remember when we see it."

"Well, girls," Mom said, "I think we're going to grab some lunch before we head over to Aunt Celia's house and start cleaning it out."

Later, as we walked into Aunt Celia's room, I remembered the thrill and anticipation I felt before going over to see her and the wonder that coursed through my body when Aunt Celia sat us in her lap and told us stories of magic. Amina and I smiled together, recalling Aunt Celia's free spirit.

Even in her old age, Aunt Celia dressed in brightly colored clothing, bangle bracelets, colorful lipstick, and exotic jewelry. She loved, in her words, to "travel as the wind takes me." When she had free time at home, she would go into her sunroom and set up her art canvas and paints, and while she waited for inspiration to strike, she would put her hair up in these big butterfly clips and tuck her paintbrush behind her ear. I smiled, remembering her bubbly personality and bright smile that went right along with it.

"Can you grab the key on her dresser?" I asked Amina, who was standing next to me.

She reappeared beside me a moment later, key in hand.

I slid open the closet door. Inside was a green, velvety looking chest with a thin layer of dust on it.

"Whoa," Amina breathed. "What do you think is inside?"

"I don't know. I wish we could open it now," I replied, crouching down to pick up the box from the floor. I ran my hands along the chest, trying to picture what was inside. It was about the length of a folder, and I foolishly started fantasizing about maps filled with clues leading to buried treasure.

"Stop that," I told myself. "*Don't be* silly." But I allowed my imagination the freedom to run wild, dreaming about jewels and other goods.

Amina sighed and said, "I guess we should go help everyone. Meet me in my room with the chest when we get home."

I nodded. "Can't wait," I said.

After several hours of sorting items and moving boxes, our family headed home where Amina and I were finally able to open Aunt Celia's chest.

"This definitely has my curiosity," Amina said as we sat cross-legged on the floor of her room.

I set the chest in front of us. "Do you have the key?" I held out my hand, and she dropped the cold piece of metal into my palm. I took a deep breath. "Moment of truth," I said, "Are you ready?"

Amina nodded. "The suspense is killing me. Open it!"

"Okay! Okay!" I inserted the key into the keyhole and turned it, the room so quiet Amina could probably hear my heart beating. I opened the lid and...

"Her paintbrushes?" Amina's face fell. "All of that fuss over her paintbrushes?"

"Maybe she cherished her paintbrushes more than we thought?" I mused.

"Yeah... but something doesn't add up," Amina said as she picked up one of the paintbrushes and examined it.

"Um, what are you doing?" I asked.

"I'm checking to see if there's something about the paint-brushes that could give us clues as to why she gave us these."

"Oh, good idea." I picked up another paintbrush and studied it, looking for words or pictures or any clue at all.

"I can't find anything," I told Amina a few minutes later, putting down the shimmery brush.

"Yeah, me neither," she replied, looking defeated.

"Hey," I told her, "don't give up. Let's check the box. Maybe a note from her fell under the cushion."

"Maybe," she said, sounding doubtful.

I took out the cushion and felt along the bottom, searching for loose paper. "I don't feel anything-wait! A corner of the velvet lining on the bottom of the chest is loose!"

Amina's face briefly lit up, before quickly falling again. "The box is probably just old."

"No," I replied, excitement in my voice. "There's something under the lining!"

Amina jumped up. "What is it?" she asked.

I peeled back the lining and picked up a leather-bound book.

"Whoa," Amina breathed. "What is it?"

"I don't know," I said, stroking the soft leather of the book.

"Well, let's read it!" Amina craned her neck to better see the book.

I opened it and squinted to see the writing on the inside front cover, which read:

Property of Celia Andrews

The next few pages were filled with faded writing:

Oh, Diary! Here I am in the m*agnifique* city of Paris! And what a marvelous day I've had. I've seen the beautiful sights, eaten the delicious food, and done the greatest of shopping! I went into the most peculiar of shops, today. At first, I wasn't even sure if it was a shop at all. It was nestled in between two other storefronts and the sign above the door was so faded and dusty I could barely make out what it said. When I opened the door, a bell jingled and an elderly man came rushing forward to welcome me in French. Noticing my American accent, he quickly switched to English. "Welcome to *Monsieur* Alain's Art!" he greeted me, "I am *Monsieur* Alain. Is there anything I can help you find today?" I smiled politely and straightened my shoulders, trying to act sophisticated. After all, not many nineteen-year-olds get to spend their summer break in Paris, and I don't want to mess it up by acting too childish. "*Bonjour, Monsieur.* I am just looking around, thank you." I replied.

The shop was filled with gorgeous works of art, and my being an artist myself, I felt as if I were right at home. "*Monsieur*, this art is *magnifique!*" I told him, marveling at the rolling hills and other beautiful landscapes. "*Merci, Mademoiselle*," *h*e replied, looking pleased. "Would you like to," he paused for a moment, trying to find the right words, "create art?"

I smiled. "I'd love to."

After he set out the canvas and paint supplies he stepped back. "What do you want me to paint?" I asked him.

"Oh, just paint what the paintbrush calls you to," he said, and he gave me a wink. I wasn't sure what he meant, but I tried to do what he said.

Once I was done-minutes later- I set the shimmery brush down and looked up from the stool where I was sitting. "*Monsieur*, I think I am done."

His eyes shone. "Oh, *Mademoiselle*, It is m*agnifique!*"

I blushed from his praise as I looked at my painting of the streets of Paris. "*Merci, merci, Monsieur,*" I replied.

His eyes searched mine for a moment before he said, "Come, I must show you something." He shuffled away, and I followed him towards a door in the back of the room. I know that I should have been more careful before following a stranger into a secluded room, but something told me that I could trust him. "Don't worry, you can trust me." He said, reading my mind. He took a deep breath and continued, "When you first stepped into my store, I could see that you had a heart of gold, and if you don't know, those are so hard to find. I'm going to explain something to you, and you might be confused, but please humor me."

Although it was hard to understand him through his thick accent, I smiled and nodded for him to go on.

"I know you may think that I am a silly old man, and that this is a silly old store, but there is so much more to the story."

He went on to explain that the store was around when he was a child, and one day he stepped into it and met a mysterious old woman who later told him the same things he was telling me. He said that there is an organization with different locations around the world, and they help those in need. He explained how certain people get the "gift" to see and seek out those in need. Those in the organization are always seeking out those who possess the "gift," specifically artists because sometimes their gifts come out through their art. I asked him to elaborate on this, as I didn't understand what exactly this meant. He told me, as an example, that a painting may show you a person or place where someone is in need.

"This organization is something only very special people are chosen for, and it is not for the faint of heart," *Monsieur* Alain said, looking me in the eyes intensely.

"So, you're saying that I possess this gift?" I asked, "How can you tell?"

He smiled kindly. "Trust me; I can tell."

My eyes filled with tears, and I ran up to him and enveloped him in a hug, temporarily forgetting about trying to act sophisticated. He chuckled. "My dear girl, you're going to break my ribs." I let go and smiled at him.

"Come," he told me. "I have to show you something."

I followed him out to the room where I had painted, and we stopped by his art canvas. He picked up a velvety box on a shelf and opened it. "This was the box the woman gave to me when I stumbled upon this store, and now I want you to have it."

I stroked the box first, running my fingers on the velvet and then moving from the silk pillow nestled inside to the beautiful paintbrushes sitting on top. "Oh, *Monsieur*, how can I ever thank you?" I asked softly.

"My dear," he said, "I should be thanking you. I've spent many years of my life trying to find someone like you, and now I can finally rest, knowing that I have. Besides, I'm getting a little old for the organization, anyway." He winked at me, and I thanked him again. "*Merci, Monsieur* Alain. Will I ever see you again?"

His eyes twinkled. "I have a feeling we'll be running into each other again. But until then, *au revoir!*"

As I headed towards the door and called out, "*Au revoir!*" in reply, a question struck me like a bolt of lightning: "But Monsieur Alain, when I find someone in need, how will I know how to help?"

I turned around to hear his answer, but he was nowhere in sight. It was as if he had disappeared into thin air.

And now, Diary, I must go to sleep, for it is very late. Goodnight, or should I say, "*Bonne nuit!*"

"Whoa," Amina said, staring at the journal in disbelief. "I can't even believe this."

"I know," I replied, trying to process what we had just read.

"Is there more?" Amina asked.

I flipped through the book. "I don't think so-wait, there's something on one of the last pages."

In more of Aunt Celia's writing, this was written:

Clever girls, I knew you would figure it out. I'm sorry that I had to be so tricky, but if all of this information gets in the wrong hands, it would be very bad. Now, let me explain all of this to you:

I saw something in you girls, just like *Monsieur* Alain saw something in me. You two possess the "gift," and I could tell this from when you two were very young, much too young to understand all of this. Now, I know that you are still quite young, but I know that you two are very capable girls. There is so much I haven't explained, but I could fill this whole book with explanations, and there would still be more questions you wish to ask, the biggest one being, "What will we do when someone in need is revealed to us?" To this question I say, "Trust your instincts, for the answer will reveal itself to you as the need arises." I wish I could tell you all of this in person, but we make the best out of what we have, right?

Don't you girls ever forget that I love you very much, and I have complete faith in you.

Love forever,
Celia Andrews

Amina looked at me with a thousand feelings mixed into her expression: pride, happiness, fear, sadness, wonder, and so much more. "So, Aunt Celia saw this gift in us?"

I nodded uncertainly. "I guess so."

"This is so much to wrap my head around," she said.

"I know. I feel the same way, but I also feel happy and proud that Aunt Celia saw this in us." I replied, "And a little bit afraid, too. I mean, how will we know when someone is in need?"

"This is a big responsibility," she added.

We continued to talk about Aunt Celia, her past, and our futures.

"Well, there's never a dull moment in our lives," Amina said a few minutes later.

"That's for sure," I agreed, "and I think we can both safely say, after today, that our lives will never be the same again."

Jonas Carlson

Fall 2023 Antrim Raising Writers

INSTRUCTOR INTRODUCTION: FALL 2023 ANTRIM RAISING WRITERS

David Hornibrook

We began class with the idea that language is a powerful tool to shape the way we see the world. What did we do with this serious idea? We tried to have as much fun as possible! This class was really about trying new things, giving ourselves problems to solve, and making new things out of words. And these students exceeded all my expectations.

As a poet, I found myself challenged to think a lot about fiction, since many of our students were interested in writing stories. One of my favorite activities was when we wrote a character doing a very ordinary task like putting books in a locker or baking bread and then re-wrote introducing different problems (earthquake!). The results were creative, hilarious, exciting, scary, and most of all fun.

Students, thank you for making this such a memorable experience. Your insight and enthusiasm was wonderful to witness and I learned a lot from each of you. As you continue writing, don't forget to experiment and use your mistakes as opportunities to create something new!

MISSING
Eden Henderson, fifth grade

I was at the police station. I was scared and lonely. With a police officer yelling at me.

"Who are you?! Who did this?! I've had enough, tell me where they are. If you don't who will?"

"Fine," I said *furiously. "I don't have a family …I don't know where they are." All I knew was that nothing would ever be the same.*

CHAPTER 1

I was walking with a big smile on my face. It was finally summer break. The air was fresh, everyone bloomed with glee. Green was everywhere as if someone had painted the grass, the trees so green that you couldn't tell leaf from leaf. And the roads were packed with cars driving away from the ninety-degree heat, but it was truly a nice day in Eau Clair Wisconsin "How could anything go wrong? It's a beautiful day, no one's fighting" I told myself. Then I heard a voice. My best friend Tin was right behind me. We both laughed hard, surprised to see each other. Tin had brown shady hair with brown church pants to go with it. Then I saw Harold in the distance. Harold had been Tin's enemy ever since he broke Tin's slugger action mini figure, the coolest toy in the world. There Harold was, with a group of boys. All I knew about them was that they had one thing in common: they liked to start fist fights. As Harold walked past them, Tin made a smoldering face. I could tell they were enemies without a single doubt. I decided to walk home away from Tin who was probably going to start a fight with Harold. The sky was turning dark, the green grass was growing invisible as evening came on and the traffic was all gone.

CHAPTER 2

When I finally got home the wood creaked as I walked upstairs to where my sister had a specialty of somehow squirting toothpaste on the counter. Soon I went to my bedroom decorated with models of spaceships and books about science. I slowly went to bed and laid down and as usual went to sleep fast. I had a strange dream. I heard laughing, someone grabbed me, pulled me into a chest, and locked me inside. I did not see or know the person. Then I woke up. I immediately ran out of my bed and downstairs until I ran into my dad who was making breakfast in the kitchen. "Wow slow down buddy," said dad.

"You must be excited, Peter," said mom.

"Alright get ready for summer school," said dad. So, I got ready for summer school. I got my backpack on from the doorway, ate breakfast and changed clothes. When I was ready, I got into my mom's car and she drove me to summer school.

CHAPTER 3

After summer school it was almost like the day was a page copied right off the printer. I walked home again with Tin which was only on Tuesdays. Tin made a face at Harold again. Later I sat on my bed confused. Maybe I did repeat the day. I glanced at my phone on my dresser. I stared in disbelief. I did repeat the day. I sat on my bed in shock. I was so shocked that I sat on the bed till I fell asleep.

CHAPTER 4

When I woke up, I went downstairs to get breakfast, but Dad wasn't there. I checked my mom and dad's room but neither of them where there. Then I ran to my sister's room to see if my sister was there, but she wasn't. I was scared and lonely. I was worried about them so decided to report the case to the police station. As I ran out the door to the police station, past the stores, past the houses. I did not see a single person. When I got to the police station there were no police anywhere. "Hello" I said, "is anyone here?" Desks were broken and papers were everywhere. Then someone grabbed me by the hand. I was about to scream, but he covered my mouth and dragged me by a broken police officer desk. "Quiet" whispered the police officer. "Who are you?! Who did this?!" "I've had enough, tell me why you're here or... If you don't tell me, who will?" "Fine," I said furiously.

"I don't have a family ...I don't know where they are." Then I realized I was here to find out what was going on "What's going on?" I whispered. "Aliens are attacking I just saw them dragging people into the spaceship "said the police officer. "Attacking" I yelled. "Shh, I said to be quiet," whispered back the police officer. Then the police officer looked around "Where are your parents?" he said. I said, "I don't know." "Of course, you don't know, everybody has gone missing. I was a witness. The police officer seemed to be in a grumpy mood like it happened all the time. "Everybody has gone missing, one by one. I was a witness", he said. He looked around, there I looked outside it was misty and cold there were no signs of racoons getting into the trash as usual. Then out of the corner of my eye I saw a spaceship. A dirty silver spaceship with a green line around it and a bunch of windows on the top. Finally, I told myself "Some inspiration" there I ran into the spaceship the police officer chased after me. I ran into the spaceship to see if anyone was in there. Once I was insided, the spaceship it began to hover and shake and finally rose. It swept from side to side and up and down fire began to blast at the windows of the space. Till all you could see was black with stars all decorating the black sides.

As we went up the air began to get thinner and thinner until we couldn't breath. "I can't breathe," I told the policeman. "I know me too," said the policeman. I began to slowly fall asleep. The policeman began to yell at me, "wake up wake up!" he yelled. But then he slowly begin to fall asleep. After a little bit of time, I woke up. But the police man was still asleep. I was lying almost on a hospital bed with a breathing mask on me. Everywhere was white and seemed like a hospital room. I saw one little girl and one little boy.

CHAPTER 5

The boy and girl were both talking in a language I've never seen or heard. Then the boy took off the breathing masks. For some reason I could breathe. I got up, and tried to sneak out where the doorway was, when they weren't looking. But then they turned around, "stop," yelled the girl.

I froze there scared. "It's okay" said the boy. "Then why am I even here?" I spoke in a confused voice. "She can tell you that" said the boy.

"Hello," she said, "my name is Ally." "Me and Arkin have been researching humans ever since our planet died in an asteroid shower. We found out that your planet has an atmosphere. That means that most asteroids burn up before they hit earth's surface."

"Whole different question, but why can I breathe if I basically fainted when I got on the spaceship."

"We have found that if we absorb air into your lungs that you can breathe for a certain amount of time. It depends on how much air we give you and how you can handle our spaceship. "Okay," I said.

"Okay, then you're aliens?" I spoke. "Yes, we are," said the boy. "Why are people going. missing on our planet?" I said. "It's because we have wanted company ever since our planet died." "We needed someone to take care of us, so we robbed people one by one to see if they would accept us even though we are aliens." "But not one did." She paused for a moment. "We lost everything that day". I saw a tear go down her cheek. "But we kept going. We stood up and kept going and going. Even if we fell, we got right up, and kept going, and we'll keep going until someone accepts us for who we are," said the girl.

"They never seem to accept us just because we could be a threat to society" said the boy in an annoyed voice.

CHAPTER 6

Then the boy looked at the girl, making sure she wasn't mad for telling such a thing.

"Yes," said the girl, consoling herself, "I'm okay". She wiped her tears away. The boy turned to me.

and started. Tears filled his eyes, but he didn't cry.

"I'm sorry that happened to you," I said. It was silent for a moment. But then the policeman ran off the bed and pulled off his mask.

"Freeze!" he shouted he stranded right by me ready to charge.

"Don't hurt us," cried the girl.

"Stop," I yelled. And the policeman stopped. All he did was stare.

"Is he okay?" asked the boy.

"I think so," I said.

"I think he is just scared," said the girl.

She went to him. "Hello," she said, "My name is Ally."

CHAPTER 7

"Are you aliens?" said the policeman.

"Yes," said the girl. The police man slowly began to back away. "It's okay," said the girl, "remember when you couldn't breathe, we helped you so now you can breathe. We helped you, me and my brother did. We are here because our planet has died by an asteroid shower, and we need some-one to take care of us." The girl paused for a moment, then she said, "will you?"

CHAPTER 8

The policeman hesitated and then said, "Yes". "But one condition: you have to live on earth and adopt earthly ways. Got that? You better mean it." The children chirped like birds with glee. I smiled as I watched them laugh to a happy start.

Then I fell to the ground, my glasses fell off. The children turned around. I heard voices and screams and yells and shouts. It was all like a dream. When I woke up, I was in my bedroom on the ground, with The boy and girl Looking at me. The girl breathed for a moment and then said, "OK, you're all right."

I said, "but how can you breathe". I began to freak out but then the girl said fast, "we have lungs that can absorb anything."

"What?" I said.

"Well, it's complicated", she said.

"Fine, if you can't tell him then I will," said the boy. Then the girl spoke in a language I've never heard before "yum lo mum du lee men," said the boy. Then the boy turned to me "It's because are lungs can absorb any kind of toxic air to you humans." Then the girl and boy turned to the police officer who was sitting on my bed "yum loe en ech pu lee tee en. In our language, that means: thank you for excepting us" they both said together.

Then, all of a sudden, one by one, the missing people started reappearing. All the people were back, buzzing like bees. I ran downstairs out of the door to the crowd of people. Then I started seeing my friends and my family. Soon I saw Harold talking. "what" I told myself in amassment then Tin turned running to me.

"Fixed it with Harold "said Tin in a lame voice

"you did what?" I said

"yah we thought it was better than being trapped in a stinky spaceship, but I better catch up with my mom she's probably looking for me after being trapped for about 24 hours. Anyway, bye" said Tin as he ran away. This was truly the best summer ever, no boring old me anymore, time for a fresh start.

THE END

CAPTURED
JuJu Pine, seventh grade

Silvia's eyes welled with tears that blended in with the freezing rain drops that pierced her skin. She never meant for this to happen. She just wanted her mom back. Not get her and her friends captured. A wave of guilt washed over her. Julie, Molly, Lucy, and Sarah were the only friends Silvia ever had. And now, because of her, they were going to die. As the guards dragged her by her arms, her feet scraped the grated metal floor and she caught a glimpse of Execution Arena, surrounded by the tall buildings of the market square. That was where the guards were taking them. Every second they inched closer and closer to death. They were just passing the market place, cobblestone streets crowded with people. Why did Silvia buy that lavender dress without checking for trackers first? Was buying a dress in her moms favorite color worth getting both herself and her friends killed? Her hope and stupidity had killed them all. Silvia had planned for any possible situation if they were ever captured. Except for this one. "I'm so so sorry guys." She whispered to her friends. She had expected them to look mad, sad, or betrayed. Instead, they looked...

Kind of excited.

"It is okay." Julie said reassuringly. Silvia thought that was weird but she had bigger things to worry about. Like the fact that they had arrived at the arena. She thought that things couldn't possibly get any worse. It didn't seem like they could anyway. But she was proven wrong when she saw a guard lining her mom up with the rest of her friends on the big stage in the otherwise empty room. She expected to be lined up too but she was kept where she was at. The guard controlling her must have known what she was thinking because he leaned in and whispered, "You'll get your turn up on the stage. But first, we want you to watch all your friends and family die so you learn the consequences of betraying the king." If her hand weren't cuffed she would probably have punched him. Her face must have shown it too, because the guard laughed in her face. Another guard walked over to where her mother and friends were lined up. Julie was the first in the line. Next to her was Sarah. Then Molly, Lucy, and Silvia's mom. Right before the guard shot Julie, she yelled "GO!" She slipped out of the handcuffs and rolled over, tripping the guard, causing him to drop two keys. Molly and Lucy, who had also gotten out of the handcuffs, each grabbed one. Molly ran to Silvia's mom and unlocked her hands. Lucy ran to Silvia and did the same. It had taken Sarah longer to get uncuffed, but when she did, she took the gun from the unconscious guard. Julie began to run out of the arena followed by Silvia and her mom, Molly, and Lucy. Sarah followed too but she was protecting them from guards that were trying to prevent them from escaping. They darted out the south entrance that went back to the market. They sprinted through the city knocking into people and trampling whatever was in their path. They would not be captured again. It seemed like there was an entire army chasing them. And maybe there was. The king had made it pretty clear he wanted his wife and stepdaughter dead. Silvia had told her friends very little. She should have told them more so they could protect themselves. "Scatter and meet at the base!" Sarah yelled when the guards started getting closer. They dashed in separate directions. Silvia went with her mom because only the five young girls knew the location of the secret base. The guards had mostly come after Silvia and her mom. Probably because they were the king's wanted family. The guards were too fast. Silvia and her mom were getting slower. When the guards were less than ten feet away, a group of villagers got in their way. They were helping wanted royals get away, they must have recognized the pair. It was treason. Silvia was so distracted by their sacrifice that she hadn't continued running. Her mom, who was previously behind Silvia, had passed her and didn't realize silvia had stopped until one lady shouted

"Run! We don't believe the king's lies! Go somewhere safe!"

"Thank you." Silvia whispered as her mom dragged her away towards the woods. Tears filled her eyes as she heard gunshots and screaming. She had to continue running. Finally they were able to lose the guards as they reached the edge of the forest.

The queen and princess were the last to arrive at the base that looked like an abandoned cabin.

Silvia hugged her mom for the first time in three years. Her mother couldn't talk right now because of the taciturn juice that she had been given. It would wear off in a day or two. After she let go of her mom, she went to hug her friends. "Thank you. For having a plan." She said laughing. They had made it! And next time they got captured it would be on their terms. When they were fixing the king's mistakes and taking back the throne.

FOOTSTEPS ON THE MOUNTAIN PART 2
JuJu Pine, seventh grade

Sam runs out of the cave to help Nailah, but before she gets there, someone new appears. Someone who pushes Nailah right off the edge of the mountain. The person runs off to the side and disappears into the snowy mountain air, as if they were never there. "NOOOOOOO!" Sam yells, racing to the edge of the cliff. "No." She's whispering now, spotting Nailah's bright blue designer boot. Which isn't the only thing she sees. There is also a pair of legs and lots of red.

Blood.

Sam is overwhelmed with rage and fury. Who would do this? Suddenly she hears a twig snap behind her. She turns and sees a figure in a black hooding duck behind a tree. She does not see their face, but when they speak, their voice sounds oddly familiar. "I've waited so long for this," it says. The next thing Sam knows, she too is falling, falling, falling.

"Ahhhhh!" Sam shoots up in her bed screaming. "It was just a dream!" She whispers relieved. "A stupid little dream." She looks at the clock. It's two in the morning so she decides to go back to sleep. After lots of tossing and turning, she dozes off again.

Sam finds herself in another dream. Except this time it's not angry or scary, it's sad. She is getting on a train, and her dad is standing outside. Not getting on with her. He opens his mouth to say something but all that Sam hears is Beep! Beep! Beep! Slowly she opens her eyes. Just another dream. She thinks. She jumps out of bed! It's June tenth. THE FIRST DAY OF SUMMER BREAK!!!!!!!

She runs downstairs and finds her dad making pancakes. Which isn't abnormal until she sees the chocolate chips.

Chocolate chips mean bad news.

"What's going on?" she asks, her excitement decreasing. Her dad hesitates. "Seriously!" She pushes until, finally, he says, "Fine. I have news. You are going to Missouri to spend the summer with Grandma Morgan!" He seems so happy. But Sam had to say, "Uhh. You know I've never met the lady right?"

"Yeah, but it will be fun!" He replies, going back to stirring the pancake batter. "You leave in three days."

"We. You mean we leave in three days."

Once again, her dad hesitates. When he doesn't reply, Sam says, "Nope. I'm not going. I am not going to spend the summer alone with some grandma who is practically a stranger! I won't—"

"You will. I am going on a business trip over the summer. I can't leave you home alone for three months. You are thirteen years old. Go pack."

"But—" Sam tries.

"Go. Pack."

Sam stomps up the stairs, her long, brown hair flying up behind her.

Three days roll around very quickly. Soon enough, Sam's dad takes her to the train station. After she boards, she stands at the door crying softly. She looks at her dad out the window. He opens his mouth and says, "I can't believe you are finally meeting your grandma! I've waited so long for this!" She pauses for a second. Huh. She thinks. I had a dream just like this. The train begins to pull away so Sam finds her seat. It turns out she is sitting next to a girl who is also thirteen. She looks kind of familiar. "I love your shoes!" Sam says trying to make a friend. Plus they really were nice shoes. The blue boots had to be designer or something. "Thanks!" The girl says beaming. "I'm Nailah! And you are?"

"I'm Sam." Sam replies embarrassed she forgot to introduce herself. She knows she has seen the girl's buttery blond hair, olive eyes, and blue boots somewhere before. Her mind flashes to her mountain dream. Terrified, she looks again at the boots. This is the girl from my dream. Sam is amazed. She feels sick when she hears the voice who pushed both girls off the mountain.

She recognizes it now. "I've waited so long for this!" it said. She had heard the same voice say those same words at the train station. Her face falls into her hands. She begins to cry again.

"Are you okay?" Nailah asks.

"Uh huh." Sam replies. But she wasn't. Not at all. She knew who the figure on the mountain was.

It was...

Her dad.

THE DEADLY EARTHQUAKE
JuJu Pine, seventh grade

Dahlia Monroe's footsteps echoed throughout her quiet home, just outside Traverse City Michigan, as she walked into her kitchen to make some popcorn before watching The Hunger Games, her favorite book and movie, for what had to be the two-millionth time this month.

She opened the cabinet and took out a packet of microwave popcorn and set the microwave for two minutes and thirty seconds. Her parents were at the grocery store, so she was all alone in her bug tudor style house.

In the reflection of the glass of the door, she swore she saw someone outside. She walked over to the window. She peered out, searching the darkness for any sign that someone may be lurking outside her quiet home. She was nervous for some reason. Maybe it was just a bear. Or a deer? Animals are common out in the wooded areas of Michigan. She sighed. I'm sixteen! I'm too old to be afraid of the dark. She thought, but not moving from her spot by the window.

BEEP! BEEP! BEEP!

She jumped out of her trance.

It was just my imagination. She thought. From watching The Hunger Games too much.

She opened her bag of popcorn and applied lots of salt and melted butter. She walked into the living room to search for the remote. Once she found it, she turned on the movie, sat on the couch and relaxed. Until she heard a sudden creeeeeaaak behind her. The ground shook slightly. Earthquakes in Traverse City had become more common since more oil companies were moving here. She didn't think much of it but she turned around to see if anything was there. Just as she suspected, there wasn't. She snuggled back up in her blanket and unpaused her movie. She was just getting past the introduction when there was another loud creak. Ugh.

She hoped the power wouldn't go out, sometimes the electrical lines are affected by the earthquakes. Once again Dahlia looked behind her, this time to see if any of the lights were flickering. There wasn't but, there was something there. Or rather, someone. This particular someone wore a ski mask and held an axe directly above Dahlia's head. She was frozen in shock and fear. Luckily, just before he was able to swing the axe, the ground shook again causing him to drop his weapon. The axe slid underneath the couch. Dahlia regained motion when saw her chance and made a break for the back door. When she got there,she had two options. She could run into the dense woods that were right behind the house or she could dash to her car to hide. She decided that the killer would probably think that she ran into the woods and would be able to easily find her, so she decided to go to the car and hide. While running through the yard, she hit her foot on a rock. She heard a loud crack. There was no way she could walk on it. Hear heart sunk. She rolled on her back to see how far the killer was, in order to determine whether she should try and walk or if she had time to crawl. Turns out he was close. Very close. He was right above her, with what looked like a rock in his hand. He raised his hand and then brought it down, very fast. Dahlia's final thought was the realization that she was going to die. Then the world went black. Dahlia never got to finish her movie and the bag of popcorn layed on the floor of the shaken house.

I HEAR RIVERS SINGING

Jacob Stephens, sixth grade

I hear rivers singing
with their beautiful,
resonant songs.

I listen to the creeks,
with their calming limerick of water,
to the waterfalls,
with their roaring symphony,

the ancient canyons,
with their melody as old as time,
to the young seasonal streams,
with their temporary harmonies,

to the creeks with their practiced tunes,
and the springs with their quiet melodies.

They all have a song, you just have to listen.

WIND

Fionnagan VandenHeuvel, sixth grade

The wind blows as my dogs look up with no fear
the birds chirp
the grass rustles
the plants grow beneath our feet
the trees shimmer and sway with the wind
some creak
the fallen leaves twirl into tornados

Jonas Carlson

Manistee Raising Writers

Fall 2023 Class

INSTRUCTOR INTRODUCTION: FALL 2023 MANISTEE CLASS

Lauren K. Carlson

What you're about to read is compiled from creative writing classes held at Manistee's Armory Youth Project in partnership with NWS's Raising Writers programming. Manistee—a town of 7,000 permanent residents and the historic and present homeland of the Little River Band of Ottawa Indians—is a lumber-boom town nestled between Manistee Lake and Lake Michigan. Factories line the shore of Manistee Lake, among them Morton Salt, Packaging Corporation of America and Martin Marietta Magnesia Chemicals.

Throughout their work, you'll find themes exploring the natural world, the deep feelings of adolescence, as well as long-form experiments in fantasy and horror fiction. Here you'll find several formal explorations including erasure and visual poetry. Identity and experimentation are ever-present themes for middle school and high school students. As their teacher, I'm honored to nurture the creative voices of students in my town. It's with gratitude for NWS as an organization, all our friends, supporters and readers, we share this work.

THINGS THAT MAKE TEARS FALL
Ava DeBoni, seventh grade

Grounded butterfly on the sidewalk.
Crushed robin's egg, smeared yolk.
Ice cream on the sidewalk.
Ripped and scribbled book.

The fawn on the side of the highway.
The moving truck in your best friend's driveway.
The necessitous woman asking for food.
In the cemetery fresh grass grown.

The little girl crying on the breaking news.
The car inflamed.
The hospice nurse's last moment with her client.
War.

WHERE?

Fable Wisseman, eighth grade

Tell me.
Find me.
I'm here.
Am I?
I'm not.
Who says?
Tell me.
See me.
Not here.
How so?
I am.
Stop now?
Tell me.
Show me.
Here.

HAND PAIN

Grace Condon, ninth Grade

A tree. Another tree. More trees. Swing made
with a cooler lid. The rope melted and tied in
a knot to hold it. An old worn out falling apart
rusty trampoline. Stinky, nasty deer head.
Bees. Many ants. I used to make a triangle
with my hands and catch the ants and then
kill them for fun. My brothers would rip the butts
off of the ants and eat them. I would also bike
and rollerskate down this hill. I fell and hurt
my hand. You know when you fall on cement?
And you can feel the rocks and skin ripping
off your palms. That stuff hurts for real.

FEAR & LOVE
Marlee Hamilton, seventh grade

I'm scared of

relationships. When
someone who isn't
your family says "I love you."

People, people when
they come too
close.

Getting abandoned by somebody
I love

*

I love

getting to see the people
I love.

Writing basic little
poems on my phone
or on a piece of paper.

Going on late night
walks with friends.

OCTOBER, MANISTEE COUNTY

Leah McClellan, ninth grade

The trees fighting the wind
Gravity defeating leaves
People in sweaters
Conquering hiking trails
Photo albums being taken over
Red, orange and yellow flashing by
Apple cider being number one
Gathering wood just to burn it
Fires wrapping people in warmth
Strolling down streets just for treats

NOT HAVING A TRUCK/CAR
Xander Lewis, ninth grade

Can't drive places
Can't see old faces

Never on time
Always need oil

So that engine don't spoil
Not being able to pick up friends

Can't hangout
So we need to walk

To each den
Can't go mudding

Like what the fudding
Can't travel

Feels like you move
Slow as a truck full of gravel

#1985

Pandora Escartin Ortega, eleventh grade

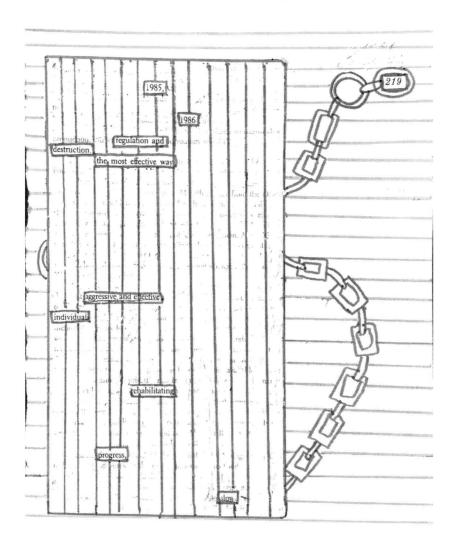

LIFE IN BALANCE

Thomas Racine, seventh grade

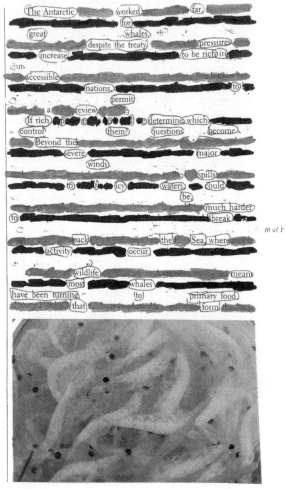

The Antarctic worked far, great for whales despite the treaty pressures increase to be rich in accessible nations to permit a review If rich control them? determine which questions become Beyond the severe winds major icy waters spills could be much harder to break pack the Sea where activity occur. wildlife most whales means have been turning that to primary food form

A relief from the Bay of Fundy.

Jonas Carlson

2024 Winter Antrim
Raising Writers

INSTRUCTOR INTRODUCTION: 2024 WINTER ANTRIM RAISING WRITERS

David Hornibrook

A series of technical problems got us off to a rocky start but this small and generous group had a lot of patience and soon we fell into a good rhythm. Each week we explored a different poetic element (language, metaphor, line, image, etc.) but our main goal was to follow the jazz composer Sun Ra's advice: "when music is in your heart, you can't do anything wrong. So why don't you make a mistake and do something right." I got a few quizzical expressions from time to time but these students were never afraid to try new things. And often with stunning results!

This was a very impressive group. Over and over, I found myself surprised, delighted, and moved by the work they did. As each of you continue to write I hope you will continue to be curious and open to surprise. The creative effort and sense of wonder I saw in each of you was inspiring!

PERHAPS
Jacob Stephens, sixth grade

It sat
upon a shelf

or maybe lay
under a bed

forlorn and forgotten
gathering dust

or possibly it
was left untouched

it could hold the
allowance

of a five year old
or the life savings of

a child but
whether it holds

change or memories
no one knows

Jonas Carlson

2024 Winter Manistee
Raising Writers

INSTRUCTOR INTRODUCTION: 2024 WINTER MANISTEE RAISING WRITERS

Lauren K. Carlson

What you're about to read is compiled from creative writing classes held at Manistee's Armory Youth Project in partnership with NWS's Raising Writers programming. Manistee—a town of 7,000 permanent residents and the historic and present homeland of the Little River Band of Ottawa Indians —is a lumber-boom town nestled between Manistee Lake and Lake Michigan. Factories line the shore of Manistee Lake, among them Morton Salt, Packaging Corporation of America and Martin Marietta Magnesia Chemicals.

Throughout their work, you'll find themes exploring the natural world, the deep feelings of adolescence, as well as long-form experiments in fantasy and horror fiction. Here you'll find several formal explorations including erasure and visual poetry. Identity and experimentation are ever-present themes for middle school and high school students. As their teacher, I'm honored to nurture the creative voices of students in my town. It's with gratitude for NWS as an organization, all our friends, supporters and readers, we share this work.

PARTY HAT

Leah Cutler, seventh grade

                              My

                    party   hat

               decided   it

          was   time

        it   was now

      a   mountain

looking   over the sun

  not   knowing

what   is going on

  it   is

  a   tree bursting

with   confetti

ENVY

Kaitlynn Hawkins, tenth grade

My sister's dances are smooth as butter,
with no sharp edges, like broken glass.

Every pirouette and arabesque, like a bird's
wings cutting through the wind.
Her hair flowing like leaves on a tree,
her hands perfectly formed.

I am quite jealous of her grace
and how freely she moves.
I do not make my jealousy known, however

for she does not envy me
the way I do.

THE THING
Nic Krause, eighth grade

When you walk in the dead of night
Don't go looking for it or you're in for a fright
Its eyes are hollow as tubes
Its face imposes a sudden doom
Its ears will make you question
If by looking you have learned your lesson
And if you start to run
It will make sure your life is done
So reader beware
This creature with claws on each finger
Will end your life and not linger

THE CREEK

Thomas Racine, seventh grade

A small little town,
There was a creek.
Many kids play there
all days of the week.
It was perfect,
once the day began.

Places to see, treats to eat
so many people to meet.
Dig a hole, toss a ball,
everyone is welcome,
both short and tall.

Here at the creek
we like to have fun,
but just wait,
the story has
only just
begun!

THE MYSTERY OF LIFE

Thomas Racine, seventh grade

How life came to be,
always evaded me.

Plants will grow
yet we don't know
how they came to be?

Animals roam,
on earth we call
home,
yet we don't know,
how they came to be?

Though we are lucky,
that we're even here,
it's still a mystery
how we came to be?

TREE
Marlee Hamilton, seventh grade

Just branches, thin branches and no leaves.
Underneath the tree, grass as I expected.
"Tree" always reminds me of evergreen trees,
but this tree is bland and lost all its leaves, just
sitting there, thin branches moving around
in the wind, looking so creepy, old and shaky.
Looking at the tree makes me miss green leaves.

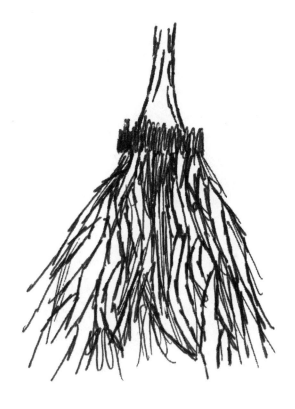

Jonas Carlson

2024 Winter Writers Create!

INSTRUCTOR INTRODUCTION: 2024 WINTER WRITERS CREATE!

Kelly Almer

The love for writing begins at an early age.

Providing opportunity for young creative minds to take their talent and passion to new and wonderful places was the purpose behind Writers Create. Our once a week class provided journal quick write time at the start of each class (I wrote with them!) and class lessons, followed by 1:1 instruction, encouragement, and support. It wasn't unusual for these writers to work on their pieces during the week, going back and forth with me in the document, discussing storyline. Their work was filled with unique and relatable characters, realistic and fantastical settings, plots that surprised and drew the reader in, and endings that brought tears of joy, heartbreak, and lessons learned. I was amazed by their talent!

Imagery, use of descriptive language, winding plots; everything imaginable came to life through their writer's visions. The young writers wrote their plot lines to create pieces worthy of an audience. Though most were over five pages in length, and many are still in the process of completing lengthy pieces, every participant deserves accolades for their dedication these past three months. I have enjoyed working with every one of them and it is my sincere hope they continue with this passion and talent.

SURVIVAL
Annabelle Weinrich, fourth grade

Clara Smith is a rich snobby kid who has nothing to do except watch survival shows on her own mini television. But when she goes on a dreaded camping trip and gets lost on the trail she has to use all of her knowledge of the outdoors to survive. She is not a wildlife person and when she encounters a bear she learns a lesson the same with the fish and her injury and so on. After spending a few days in the wild it has made her a scabbed up tough land girl that no longer dreams of her gourmet spaghetti meals at home. She is a new person, a brave person and has learned a lot from her time with the wild. Now she prefers to spend her weekends not just going to the mall and has the forest to thank for that.

THE STORM
Lily Wagner, fifth grade

Weeds swayed beneath the glassy surface while the comforting hum of bugs hung in the air. The slick canoe paddle glided across the smooth water and planted itself deep in the cool still lake. A Loon cried over the still surface, its call echoing over the lake. The call seemed sad and lonely but also happy. Christy breathed in the deep, piney scent of the woods, it filled her nostrils as she paddled back to shore. It was evening, and all the others were sitting at the fire roasting marshmallows over the hot crackling flames.

"How was the canoe going out on the lake? It looked pretty calm" Dad commented while sipping his tea.

"Good" Christy replied. "I heard a Loon in the distance. It was really cool"

"I think I heard it" added Christy's younger brother Wallace. He was seven years old.

"You sure did," said Mom while wrestling with Emma, Christy's three-year-old sister trying to pry her from her face. "Woon?" Emma questioned

"Want a marshmallow?" Dad tossed the bag to Christy.

"Absolutely!" she replied.

While Christy sat on her log she gazed into the wild orange flames reaching for the air. Loud peaceful crackling came from the tree resin on the sticks they had to scrounge for in the forest.

Suddenly she realized that the marshmallow she was roasting was on fire! "Aww man!" moaned Christy.

"I'll eat it!" shouted Walace. "I like them that way. See!" he bit into his own charred black marshmallow "Mmm, delicious"

" Here" Christy, "you can have mine".

"Marmow?" mumbled Emily. Everyone laughed at this one.

"Well I think it's time to head to bed" said Dad "You think so Carol?" "Yes I think it is".

"Nooooo I don't wanna" whined Walace.

"Come on, let's brush our teeth and put out the fire," Dad replied. Christy grabbed a jug of water and poured it over the hot fire, watching hot steam rise billowing in the air.

As a tradition Christy's family did this each year in the warm early fall, roasting marshmallows over the hot fire and sleeping outside in a tent.

Christy loves to camp.

Once everyone had eaten their breakfast, Wallace wanted to go swimming "Hey Mom can we go swimming today?'

"Of course the lake is right there you know"

"Yay!" Yelled Walace.

"Ok first things first" said Dad. "Who wants to get dressed?"

"I will" said Walllace.

Once everyone was dressed they grabbed their towels and ran to the lake. The cool water felt good on Christy's legs. She ducked under the surface and opened her eyes. She saw the soft sand littered with sticks and acorns. A little turtle swam by and a crowd of minnows swam under her feet. She looked at the weeds swaying in the deeper water and in the shallows she saw pine cones scattered on the sand. Christy emerged from the water with growling sounds. "WATER MONSTER!" yelled Wallace. "SWIM!"

"It's ok,"it's just me." she laughed.

"THAT WAS NOT FUNNY" yelled Walace . Emma gave her a suspicious look then mumbled, "Chwisty?"

"Yes, it's just me," said Christy.

"Cwisty!" Emma yelled swimming towards her but her floaties wouldn't let her.

"It's ok,"she said , swimming towards her. Emma giggled as she ducked under the water and tickled her feet. "Be careful you don't want her to swallow some water and choke" Mom cautioned "Ok." she replied.

Suddenly a loud clap of thunder rumbled across the sky echoing in the trees and bouncing off the ground. Emma whimpered and Walace looked scared. Huge rolling clouds ate the puffy white ones. They devoured the sky, eating it as if it were a wolf attacking a lamb. A bright flash shone through the clouds giving it an enhanced look.

"I-I think we should probably get out of here" Mom commented nervously, still gazing at the clouds. Christy scooped up Emma and brought them to shore. "Go get in the car." said Mom as she helped Dad hurriedly put the tent away.

"The radar says that we have a severe storm coming in." He said

But that wasn't the worst of it.

Soon hail pelted them and rain fell down hard... hard enough to not be able to see ten feet away from her. "I have to go help them" Christy said as two disfigured silhouettes moved around frantically in the hard rain. Christy jumped out of the car and Emma started crying as Christy ran towards the figures.

"CHRISTY!" yelled Mom because it was so loud. " GET BACK IN THE CAR!" "IT'S TOO DANGEROUS!"

"NO!" she yelled back "I NEED TO HELP YOU"

"CHRISTY" yelled Dad. "TAKE THIS BAG TO THE CAR" he said as he tossed a heavy duffel bag to Christy. She staggered under its weight and walked blindly to the car or so she thought.

Why haven't I arrived at the car yet? She thought as she put the bag down.

Christy walked in a circle trying to retrace her footprints. She couldn't hear anything through the noise of the elements.

Then it hit her; "No no no this can't be happening! I can't' be lost?" She said as tears sprang to her eyes and she felt a sob rise in her throat. She must stay calm, she thought. I need to think. What can I do to help? I'm not anywhere near the car.

Where was it?

Where was everyone? Were they all okay? How were Wallace and Emma? Were Mom and Dad hurt? She started panicking.

I can still find them, Christy thought to herself. I'm not far from them... I think. But still I need to get back. Ugg. This day is turning out to be horrible.

The winds soon got worse and lightning flashed brightly in the sky making it seem like noontime. The rain only came down harder and the trees shook as the wind swayed wildly. A sob forced its way out of Christie's throat and escaped her mouth. She stood there wet and desperate, mud covered her clothes and pine needles stuck to her skin. I should have stayed in the car, she thought.

Flashbacks of when she was small hit her from when she'd get upset and her mother or father would help her

"NO NO NO!" She kept saying this in her head and the words helped calm her. She felt stronger.

"I am brave." She said this again. She got up and started walking in the downpour. Now which direction do I go in? she thought. I don't know! How would I know? Ugggg! She thought to herself. She needed to rest.

As she lay down under a tall wide low-branched white pine tree its long branches drifted over her as the storm still raged. She fell asleep, sheltered.

The next morning she woke up to a clear sky and the bright sun shining over her. She got up tired, achy and wet, her hair felt mussed and the clothes she had on muddy and wet. Somehow all the bushes and small trees stood shattered from the harsh wind and rain but the tall white pine stood strong and proud, as if showing off it had survived the storm while most small ones stood hunched and tattered over their broken limbs.

As she walked out from under the branches she heard a cry from behind her. "CHRISTY!" Someone ran into her yelling, "I was super worried! Where were you?" It was Wallace.

Christy was too speechless to speak and could only sputter.

"CHWISTY!" and then Emma cannon balled into her, hugging her.

"CAROL WE FOUND HER!" Dad said, relieved, running to Christy.

"D-D- Dad!" was the only thing she could sputter. How did this happen? She thought? In one moment, she was tired, cold and a little bit hungry. Then next she was in the safe arms of her family.

Mom came running through the woods and said,

"HOW DID YOU GET BACK?"

"B-b -back?" Christy replied then she looked behind her.

There sat the camp site, the tent was packed away and so was everything else.

But how?

She thought, "How could I have been so close to the camp site and not have known it?"

She realized that the tree was only a hundred yards away hidden behind bushes. "We had policemen roaming the woods and helicopters searching for you, and you just popped up?" Mom said, greatly relieved.

As everyone else was loading up the rest of the camping gear Christy walked over the tall strong tree and looked up at it proudly and whispered "thank you." Its branches seemed to nod in return to her. She realized the tall strong tree was like her. She stood strong in the storm. She was protected by it and she remembered her family who cared about her so much. As one she was a strong tree but together they were a whole grove of trees.

FOUND

Marin Henry, sixth grade

I hear a long, sad howl.

I whip my head up from the box I call home.

It was the new guy again. He just moved into Oakwood Avenue Alley. On the other hand, I have been in the alley my whole life, after my mom's human threw her out and she had puppies. I was the only one who survived. But I am thriving here. Sort of. I leave my box and walk over to the poor fella. "Down in the dumps bud?" I say with a yawn and a stretch. He looks at me and starts telling me the pet store story again. Before I could give an answer, Grace walked over and interrupted us.

"Have any of you seen my brush?" She asks. Grace always has a brush with her for her beautiful coat. She's an Australian Shepherd. "Well, don't just look at me, give me an answer!" She says impatiently.

"What? No, I didn't take it." I told her. She looks at Buster, who gives a little whine. She walks away. Just then, I see Christine the mini Dachshund run off with Grace's brush. I inch closer to see Christine working her stubby little legs to run away from Grace, who aggressively yells, "Give me my brush back!"

Life isn't always easy in the alley.

I turn back to Buster and give him an encouraging nod. He trots off towards the feeding cup.

I walk to the park where I know I can get free treats.

As I walk, I see a collar dog. He is harnessed and tied to a leash. The human says something and the collar dog sits. He eats a treat out of his hand and gets some pats on the head. I gag. You'll never catch me tied to a human. I quickly scamper off.

Once I get to Main Street Park, I see kids and adults alike talking and laughing. I don't look at them. I don't need a human. I am my own dog. I shake off my feelings and head to the bakery, where free dog treats are outside the door. I hop up on my hind legs and grab treats for the whole alley. I get a few looks but no one stops me. As I walk home I find a bag of cotton stuffing! I put the treats in the bag and scampered home.

"Hey, Herc," Christine says as she bounces up and down.

"Hey, Christine." I sigh. "My name is Hercules, not Herc." I groan as I set the bag down.

"Right, I remember you saying that. How did you get that name anyway?" She asks, still bouncing. I sigh again, "When I was a puppy, I was walking down by the theater to get some popcorn, and a blanket fell on me from the apartment above. Someone walked by and said, "That puppy looks like Hercules from the movie!" And my new name just stuck."

"Wow." She said, "That is a cool story!" and bounced away.

"Hey, Grace!" I yell across the alley. She wearily walks over.

"Huh?" She asks.

"I got treats for the whole alley! And I found a whole thing of cotton stuffing! We can make our boxes more comfortable!" I say with excitement.

"I'll start passing out treats and you start fluffing boxes." She replies.

I nod and get to work. I watch as Grace gently gives each dog a treat. We have seven dogs in our alley and they all have their own story. Me and Grace take care of them all. There are mostly older dogs and puppies. One of the older dogs approaches me, "Hey boy, what did you find today?" His weary voice struggles to spit out.

"I found some food and stuffing for our beds," I told him.

His name is Todd and he's the oldest of the group at 13 years. "Why don't you sit down Todd? It's almost lights out." I say.

"You're probably right boy," he says as he lays his old bones down in the box. It's about 9:30pm so I lay down in my own box after I make sure the young and the old are asleep. I slowly drift off myself.

The next morning I woke up to a moving truck. I jump out of my bed. There are humans by our alley!? I slowly inch closer to the entrance. I have made sure the group is unable to be seen from the front but you can't be too sure with humans. I stick my head out of the entrance just a tiny bit. I see people moving box after box into the abandoned store next to the alley. I sniff the air but all I can smell is car exhaust. "Hey look a dog! I think he's a stray." Shoot. I've been spotted. I run off towards the back of the alley. I can still hear their confused voices.

"Grace," I say. She looks at me with her tired eyes. "People are moving into the abandoned store," I tell her. She takes a second to process but immediately starts thinking when she does. "Maybe you should go check it out?" She finally says. I look at her like she's crazy. But I reluctantly agree.

I run up to the store. The moving truck is gone but the boxes aren't. I sneak up around the side and look into the window. There is a man inside signing papers. I sniff around and I'm greeted by the sweet smell of dog treats. I shake myself off. Without getting distracted, I must find out what is going on there. I crawl up to the door and put my nose up to it. The next thing I know the door goes crashing open and I am standing right in front of the human. He looks at me, then starts walking towards me. He shuts the door and sits on the floor. I cock my head at him. He scoots closer. He reaches out a hand and places it on my ear. Right as I was about to bite this guy, he gave me the best ear scratch I have ever had. When I snap out of it I run for the door and go back to the alley. "Where have you been!?" Grace asks, sniffing me all over. "And why do you smell like a human?" Right before I was going to give a response, Christine ran by us and started screaming, "Dog food! Someone left ALL of us dog food!" Grace and I look at each other.

We ran to the front of the alley to see that Christine was right. There were seven bowls of dog food right there. I lick my lips in wonder. I was looking around to try and see who left it when I saw the guy from the store again. "Grace," I whisper. "It's the guy." She looks over in his direction. I walk up to him cautiously. He looks at me surprised. I take a risk, lay down, and proudly put my belly up in the air. He lays his hand down on me and gives me a good scratch. My tail *thump thump thump*'s against the ground.

It felt good to be loved by someone.

I open my eyes and look back to the alley. Grace looks at me with an emotion that I can't quite recognize. I look at the human and then back at the alley. He has a soft smile and gentle, loving hands. But the alley is my home and I can't leave until I know everyone is safe. I start to slowly walk away. "I'll be back with more food tomorrow." I hear him say. He smiles. I wag my tail and run home. To the alley.

"What. Was. That." Grace says in a grave voice. I gulp. "We have a friend!" Christine exclaims. I laugh. "Yeah, we do." Grace walks away. I am all mixed up inside. On one hand, I felt so good when the human petted me. I felt loved. But on the other hand, Grace has had a bad past with humans and I don't know if I can find her a new home. I curl up in my bed and dream mixed-up dreams.

For the next few days, I ponder how to get my friends a new, loving home. Every day human comes to visit me and the alley. Giving us food and love. I found out his name is Mark. Everyone has gotten used to him and feels safe around him at this point. Except Grace. She still won't go near him. Mark has tried his hardest but he won't get her. Buster has gotten very used to him coming and is very happy for some human companionship. We all need this.

The next day Mark brings more than just food. He brings us all leashes, harnesses, and...... collars? He slides the harnesses and collars on us and clips us to the leashes. Grace refused to come out and try on her stuff. Mark sighs and takes us all up to the store. He lets us off the leashes. We all sniff around the beds and food bags. He sits on the floor and rolls toys to us. After hours we lay on the floor, panting, but happy.

We start to head to the alley, where Grace is by herself. She walks up to us but when she sees Mark she vanishes. I stay and wait for her for hours. It's starting to get late and she's not back. Right as I was about to go looking for her she walked in. I start to chew her out but she stops me. "I am ready for Mark to let me go to a home. I was at the store and found out he is running an animal rescue. And he has homes picked out for all of us. Buster, Christine, Todd, Bailey, Lila, You, and me." She says. I am processing everything. But when I do I ask: "Who am I going to?" She replies: "You are staying with Mark I think." A wave of relief goes over me. I yawn and lay down in my new bed that Mark gave us. I dream that tomorrow Mark will give everyone a home with a bed, food, water, and love. And I envision my new life waiting for me.

Sure enough, The next day Mark brings all of us, and I mean including Grace to the rescue. The same morning I told everybody that morning what Mark was planning so we were ready. When we walked in the door we were greeted with people from all over town coming to adopt us. Mark walks to the front of the room, ready to announce who will go with whom. We are all itching with excitement.

"Hello everyone!" Mark announces. "I will be giving you your dogs today! Remember, these dogs have been in the alley for at least a year. So they might be scared. Please be gentle and patient. Thank you! So for our first dog, Bailey will be going home with Mr. Smith!" I watch as Bailey bounds over to the older man who picks her up and kisses her. "For our second dog!" Mark says. "Buster will be going with Mrs. Bradley!" Buster nervously walks to the little school teacher but quickly warms up when she offers him a treat. "Now our third dog!" Mark exclaims. "Todd will be going with Docter Matt!" Todd shuffles his way over to the lab-coated doctor, waiting with his arms out. Todd gives him a big kiss and he laughs. "Our fourth dog, Lila will be going to Margret!" Lila runs over to the little old woman who is smiling from ear to ear. "Now, our last three dogs have a 3 way best doggy friendship. So the owners of these three dogs must keep them together with playdates and walks and anyway they can see each other." Mark wipes his eyes and proceeds to say: "These dogs have been through so much so let's give them loving homes." I smile in the best way a dog can. "Our fifth dog, Christine, will be going to Anna, a loving little four-year-old. Anna, she will match your energy so keep up!" Christine looks at us, licks both of our faces, runs over to the little girl, and yaps her happy little barks. "For our sixth dog, Grace will be going to Ms. Marry. A psychologist at Colorado University! Take care of her for us!" Grace cautiously walks over to her but cuddles up in her lap almost immediately. "And for our last dog, Hercules. I absolutely loved him from the second I saw him. So I will be keeping this little guy!" I jump up on him and lick his face! He laughs and after we say our goodbyes to the dogs, Mark and I spend the whole night together,

So that's where we are now. I know a few weeks ago I said you would never catch me being tied to a human. But now, I am that dog. Sitting on the curb eating treats from Mark, getting all the head pats. But when I was sitting on that curb eating treats, It clicked. It doesn't matter if you live on a curb or in a house And as I curled into my bed by the fire last night and realized how lucky I am. Some dogs stay in the alley forever. But I have Mark, Grace, and Christine. I have a home and a fireplace. I have it good. No, not good. I have it perfect.

The ~~End~~ Beginning

THE GIRL WHO DIDN'T WANT TO WORK
Natalie Gilmartin, fourth grade

Chapter One

I woke up to the sound of talking.

I was in an orphanage.

I have been here now for three years. Mom and Dad left me after Dad decided he didn't want me as his daughter. So it was just Mom and me for a while until...

Mom decided she couldn't take care of me anymore, because taxes piled up and she became poor. She didn't want me to grow up poor. I don't hold it against her for wanting me to have a better life.

Will Avery be happy in the end?

EXCERPT

A Few Months Later...

Avery was so excited she built the shelter! It was basically a shack, but it worked. It had five cages for dogs or cats with lots of toys and a little knitted blanket in each cage. They get lots of attention from Avery and her two workers, Matt and Catherine. There were three bird cages, with little toys, and two pens for horses and donkeys. She has saved about fifty animals so far.

One day, Avery came home with a tiny puppy as big as her hand. Avery's mom was sitting on their red velvet couch. Avery came up to her and sat the puppy on her lap. "What is this?!" she said looking at Avery.

"Look at them," Avery said.

Isabella took one look at them, and within a matter of seconds her heart melted.

"Awwww"... she said. Fine, okay okay I know why you showed them to me. Hop in the car let's get more of these adorable puppies." They got in the car and drove off.

In the end, her mom invested to make a better shelter and put them all around the nation.

STELLA IN THE STARS
Sophia P.

It was a long day, and Stella Starling was ready to rest. She opened the door and ran up a tall, grassy hill. She laid on her back, and breathed in the fresh flowery smell. She enjoyed the calm, quiet feeling, and let all her troubles float away as if they were inside a balloon.

Stella is a young girl who has a big imagination. She thinks she is an ordinary girl but she is special. Stella eventually learns about her past and figures out she is a special person connected to the stars. She goes on the adventure of a lifetime and learns to become a brave warrior. Read Stella in the Stars to hear more!

SEA BEAST
Soren Funk, fourth grade

Once,there were explorers and they traveled the world's oceans to protect sea creatures that were in danger. Coral,Kraken,Silda,Manak,and their fish,Cephalox were their names and they bravely answered the call. The family's passion and expertise are relied upon from every corner of the globe whenever an aquatic animal needs help. They can be relied on to rescue the injured or endangered animals. Their mission has been going on for five years and doesn't slow down or stop. Their only obstacle in this demanding work: Dr. Sea Scorpion! WIll this dangerous mastermind prevent them from saving the oceans' helpless sea creatures? Read the story, "Sea Beast" to find out!

P.S. If you want to know what happens next,wait for book two to come out with even more!

ONE WITH THE WILD
Ziva Erlebeck, fifth grade

Prologue

The cage shook as the creature inside tried to break free and get away. It seemed to be a silver fox but it was acting very strangely. It kept standing up on its hind legs and making weird paw movements that seemed almost like sign language.

The fox twitches its ear, looking annoyed and impatient and continues trying to get out of its cage.

The silver fox suddenly disappears and in its place was an American avocet bird that began to pick the large lock with its long slender beak. Sirens blared as the lock fell off with a clunk and the bird began to fly up toward the open skylight and out into the starry sky.

The following section features work by high school students, which may not be appropriate for young readers.

Jonas Carlson

Writers Studio

INSTRUCTOR INTRODUCTION: WRITERS STUDIO

Teresa Scollon

The Writers Studio program at Northwest Ed Career Tech offers a creative home and college credit for high school juniors and seniors. This is an intensive two-year creative, professional, and journalistic writing program built for students who love to write. We cover many creative and professional writing genres—poetry, nonfiction, playwriting, fiction, journalism, professional writing—as well as audio production in a collaborative, workshop-based environment. We build skills and then apply them to real-world situations. Students develop a writing portfolio, submit work to competitions, and seek publishing opportunities. Seniors may be eligible to work in an internship or job shadow experiences. Visits by published authors and other working professionals help students build a sense of the wider professional world. For more information, visit: https://www.northwested.org/career-tech/programs/writers-studio/

Many students come into the Writers Studio with a real love of fantasy fiction, but not much exposure to other genres. One of our goals is to open up a wider sense of the varied world of writing. The pieces you see here were written during the fall semester, in brand-new genres: poetry, creative nonfiction, and playwriting. We really loved the discovery of and experimenting in new forms; we hope you enjoy reading this work.

ALWAYS YOU
Hunter Arnold, eleventh grade

I got easily attached to you.
It could have been called a problem,
But I wouldn't have it any other way.
I love you more than words can express.
There isn't one single word
That could even come close to explaining
My love for you,
But I'll find the words.
I know that what I feel,
I could ramble about for eternity.
That still wouldn't be long enough.

But I'll start with your smile,
My favorite thing about you.
Your smile helps me escape that darkness.
That smile could replace the stars in the night sky.
I could go on forever about your smile.
Like how every time you smile,
It's followed by a low raspy laugh.
I love that laugh.
I love how you can make me laugh,
Especially when nobody else can.
I love it when you pull me close,
And I can hear your heartbeat with mine.
I could list a million things I love about you but I won't.

You are the first and last thing
On my mind every day.
The easiest thing I have ever done
Is choose to be yours.
I know that sounds ridiculous,
But imagine a beautiful garden of flowers.
I picked this rose.
It took a while for it to open up,
But when it did it was beautiful and perfect.
I picked you,
Out of all the other billions of roses.
I don't think I'll ever be able to hear your name
Without feeling something.

I expect a happily ever after.
That may only exist in the movies or books I read,
But you make me happy,
And that is enough.
That is everything.
As the poets say, you're half my soul.

...if I could press my lips against you again
Minnie Bardenhagen, twelfth grade

I scraped your water key on the tile
Clenched your bell braces in my clammy hands
Pressed your tuning slide against my cheek
You watched me trip on my gown, many times

I greased your valves and bathed you
As often as I could
Rested your neck on my shoulder
Let every nearby town hear your voice

My embouchure needed work
Your slide squealed past 6th position
But you still made honeyed tones
In homophonic ballads

Now you're huffing and puffing
In a dusty, cobwebbed corner
I hear you screaming at me
Through your scraped and dented mouth

And as often as I could
In a time where the world was confined
I tried to unhook the latches
But there were no sheets to read
No auditoriums with creaky stands
Or seas of beady eyes to make it all matter
But I swear

I would learn to stop bell-checking for an E flat
I would tighten the corners of my mouth
I would keep my airflow steady
I would, as often as I could...

THE LAST TIME I SAW YOU
Kaihe Brown, eleventh grade

The image is so haunting.
That long dark brick hallway
that seemingly got darker and darker the further it went,
the lone bulletin board hanging on the wall,
haphazardly covered in loose papers.

Then there was you.

You were my whole world.
In a world where everything was changing around me
you were the only thing that stayed the same,
you were the only thing I understood,
the only thing that stayed the same,
the only thing I loved.

And there you were
Police officers on either side of you,
Telling us both to say goodbye.

As we hugged for one last time
I remember I gave you a teddy bear
to keep with you while you were gone,
to keep a part of *me* with.
I still remember the tears running down your face,
Then as you turned around I remember the cops guiding you down the
hall,
your silhouettes disappearing into the dark.

What I once thought would be a small time apart,
would end up being the last time I saw you.

JACKIE ROBINSON FACED UNJUST TREATMENT

Evelyn Choate, eleventh grade

"As long as I appeared to ignore insult and injury, I was a martyred hero to a lot of people who seemed to have sympathy for the underdog. But the minute I began to answer, to argue, to protest—the minute I began to sound off—I became a swellhead, a wise guy, an uppity [censored]. When a white player did that, he had spirit. When a black player did it, he was ungrateful, an upstart, a sorehead", is what Jackie Robinson said about his time playing baseball.

In the early ages of baseball it was very segregated. It was difficult for black players to be able to join, play, and travel with white teams because of Jim Crow laws and racist attitudes, John Moore stated in his ebook *Baseball encyclopedia of Race and Racism*. Many organized baseball leagues had unofficial rules that did not allow white teams to have black players on their roster and prohibited black teams from joining their organization, according to Charles Alexander in his ebook *The Color Line in Baseball.* This is what led to the formation of the National Negro League, NNL. This division was named the color line. During this time black players were treated harshly. One player, John "Bud" Fowler, became the target of spikes and it got so bad he began having to tape pieces of wood to his legs in order to protect himself. Sometimes NNL games were even interrupted or canceled because of threats from white supremecist groups such as the KKK, Alexander also said. One player in particular who stands out during this time is Jackie Robinson.

Jackie Robinson was mistreated by many people during his time as a baseball player. Unlike his white teammates, he was not treated with respect but instead greeted with racism, according to Alexander. When Robinson joined the Cardinals, he witnessed his clubhouse manager pick up his white teammates' uniforms but then when it was time to pick up Robinson's, the manager refused to touch it and instead reached for it with a long pole. His clubhouse manager even went as far as to separate his uniform from the other players' laundry and exclusively sent it to black-owned cleaning businesses which were on the other side of town. While the Dodgers were doing spring training, they would stay at hotels where they were all accommodated to, except for Robinson. The workers refused to serve him. During the spring training trip Robinson was excluded from enjoying hotels and restaurants, he was moved to the back when the team would ride a bus, and he was even bumped from flights, according to the ebook *Breaking Baseball's Color Barrier*. Not only did he endure racism off the field but on it as well. Out on the field, pitches were thrown at his head, he was called racial slurs, there were even threats of riots . When baseball became integrated, the KKK would threaten Robinson and other black players, Jim Brown said in his ebook *Stardom and Death Threats*. The Dodgers president decided to schedule his Brooklyn team to play a game in the segregated south, which enraged KKK members. They stated they would resort to violence to prevent the game from happening. Robinson and another player, Campanella, received seven letters threatening them during the weeks before the game, according to Brown. Although Robinson went through all this, he still stayed strong, defended himself, and fought against racism. Not only was he an athlete but he was also an activist.

Jackie Robinson left behind a legacy. He was one of the first players who was able to integrate baseball. On April 15th, 1947 he became the first African American to play in the major leagues, thus breaking baseball's six decade long color barrier, Martin Stenzo acknowledged in *Jackie Robinson's Battle With Equality*. Not only was he the first African American to play in the major leagues but he was also the first African American to serve as VP of a major American corporation (Chock Full o'Nuts) and commentator for Major League Baseball. He was also on the board of the NAACP where he fought for civil rights and equality. While working for the NAACP, he would write letters of both praise and criticism to big political figures . One of his biggest efforts in fighting for civil rights was his writings, speeches, and fundraiser to help rebuild the churches burned down in Albany, Georgia. By doing this he was able to get three churches

rebuilt, according to the ebook *Robinson and the Civil Rights Movement.*
Robinson also fought racism by using his voice. In 1944, he was riding in
a U.S. Army bus when a white woman ordered him to move to the back of
the bus. Robinson refused and noted the fact that U.S. Army buses were
not segregated. This landed him in custody for disturbing the peace and
drunkenness, although he was not drunk. Eventually he was released and
found not guilty, according to Stenzo in his ebook.

Robinsons legacy continues to be honored today. In June of 1972, the
Dodgers retired his number, 42. In 1997, the MLB retired his number
on the 50th anniversary of his first game. In 2004, the MLB started recognizing April 15th as Jackie Robinson day . On April 15th they take
time to honor Robinson's life and legacy on the field before every game.
Every coach, player, and umpire wears the number 42 on his day too. In
2018, some teams started wearing a commemorative patch on their caps,
sleeves, and socks to honor him. All the proceeds from this merchandise
go towards the Jackie Robinson Foundation, according to Stenzo's ebook.

ALBA GU BRATH, I GUESS
Reegan Craker, twelfth grade

The church bell rang loud and clear over the rocky hills and mountains. A lush green rolled over the rocks and blended with the grey sky above. Serene and peaceful, the air felt light despite the ever-constant wind that flew around the mountains.

A dark hat peeked over a hill and steadily rose as the rest of the body came up with it. A man in a long, black coat trudged down the hill, hunched in on himself as he tried not to scuff his shiny black shoes on the small dirt road he was on. He was tall and bleak, sticking out against the rolling hills and mountains; a scowl could be seen on his face even from a distance. The man got closer and closer until he reached the edge of the church. He stopped, looked the church up and down and felt the large stone it was made out of before making his way again.

"John! John!" The man visibly rolled his eyes and drooped his shoulders before opening one arm to catch the flying bundle of curls and energy that was his younger cousin. He was knocked back a step by the young girl that had tied herself around his waist. She was also wearing black, a dress that went down past her knees and a slim jacket to cover her upper body from the wind. John patted her back before peeling her off of him, trying as hard as he could to avoid her.

"Hi, Sophie," he grumbled. God knew he didn't need her pestering him right now.

"You've been gone too long, John. Yer accent is all funny now. And you should have come sooner, Aunt Jenny's been worried sick about ye. Been runnin' around trying tae see if anyone knew when you'd be coming."

"I told her my flight left late," John sighed and walked faster, trying to reach the other side of the church without Sophie right next to him. Eventually he saw everyone else and contemplated turning around and heading straight back to America before anyone else could see him standing there. Before he could turn around it was already too late. He had already made eye contact with his mother and Sophie had caught up to him. Making a dramatic exhale through his nose, John waited for his mother to walk over to him and give him a tight hug around his middle. She was a small and round woman, not even able to pass his chest with a pair of heels. "Aye, you're just like your dad with that height!" his mom would always say. John kicked the memory back down into the depths of his mind.

She, like Sophie and John, was wearing black. A black knee-length dress and cardigan covered her body along with a black sun hat that was practically useless with the sun behind clouds.

"I almost thought you weren't going tae make it, Johnny. I even had them wait tae bury him for ye," she said as she pulled away from John.

"You should have just done it anyway, I told you I was going to be late," John replied.

"He sounds all funny now, donn'he, Aunt Jenny?" Sophie jumped between the two and looked at her aunt expectantly.

"Is that all you have to say about John, dear? Go off tae your mam and bother her," Jenny said. Both John and Jenny watched Sophie skip over to her mother and immediately began to chatter to her. John looked at Sophie and her mother, saw how easily they got along and saw how her dad scooped her up into a hug while holding her baby brother. His heart felt tight as he watched them and his stomach sank a little bit. How was her dad so capable of supporting two children that easily?

"Are yer gon' say goodbye? We're all waiting on you now."

The sound of Jenny's voice brought John back from his thoughts, the slight shake in it made him look back at her.

"I don't think I should, Mom," John whispered. After seeing Sophie's family close together, the thought of being at the church made his gut feel heavier by the second.

"I know it's hard Johnny, but please, it's the last time you'll ere see him." Jenny persuaded. With a groan, John hung his head in defeat and made his way to the casket that was surrounded by other family members, all dressed in black. John squeezed past the bodies and held his coat close to him so he could slink past his family members, hopefully blending into the slow-moving dark blob of bodies that stuck out against the mountains. Unfortunately, He and his father towered over everyone else in their decently sized family, so it was glaringly obvious to everyone who was passing through the crowd. John tipped his head over his face and kept his gaze down to the grass as best as he could, he absolutely did not want to speak to any more people in his family. He pointedly ignored anyone that tried to greet or console him with a sharp huff and a stern glare. John itched to go back to The States and his aunt, he didn't belong here anymore. Maybe once, when he was a young boy but that was a long time ago. He was grown and there was nothing that could change that.

When he reached the casket, John didn't even look up. He didn't want to. It's been so long, John wasn't sure if he even knew who the man in the casket was anymore. There was a noticeable hush from the crowd of people around him and John felt even more isolated from these people than he did before. The differences between him and everyone else there was too great for John to handle. He needed to get away from this place, from these people, and from the casket.

John let out a frustrated sob and turned away, rushing to find somewhere around the church that wasn't full of his family. He pulled his coat tight around him and covered his face with his mouth as he tried not to cry in front of the people he once knew when he was young. While John shove past the bundle of aunts and cousins, he accidentally pushed his mother out of the way and didn't look back as she gave him a concerned look before following him.

Eventually John found a small dip in the surrounding hills that was far enough away so he couldn't hear the rumbling murmur of voices around him but could still see the top of the church. He cried out in anger then kicked a growing chunk of tall weed that was next to him. He cried again and sat down near the kicked grass, roughly wiping his tears off with his sleeve. It was a bad idea to come here, he had work he needed to do back in America. There were more important things to do other than cry in the mountains of his hometown.

"Johnny? Johnny, are ye over here?" Jenny called from the top of the hill, behind John. He sighed and waved his hand weakly to get his mother's attention. She gasped softly when she saw the lump of black against the green and grey hills and made her way down to where her son sat in the grass.

"I thought I told ye tae say goodbye tae him, Johnny."

"He never said goodbye to me," John said as he sniffed and began to stand up again.

"Because he thought he would see ye again, Johnny! We dinnae ken this would happen!" Jenny stood up alongside her son. "He loved ye, Johnn—"

"No, he didn't, Mam! He wasnae ever there for me, even when I was young!"

"He was your father!"

"Nae, Mam! He was a father to me sisters and brothers, to the neighbor kids, to the cows even, but he wasn't a father to me. Nerre was," John's voice cracked as he got quieter, not making eye contact with his mother. She looked at John with her eyes wide, speechless at John's outburst. She'd seen him throw tantrums and other fits growing up but none of them were like this. In the back of her mind she noticed that John's accent had returned, ever so slightly.

"I'm going back to the States, Mam. There's nothing here for me. Not one thing." John's face scrunched up as he tried not to cry again. "I'll call you when I get home," he said, walking past Jenny and up towards the church to find the small dirt road. Jenny watched him go, still too shocked to pull him back to continue on with the funeral. Tears formed in both their eyes, but neither of them was able to see and neither would as long as John kept walking.

John made his way up to the dirt road and continued to walk away from the church. He could hear the faint buzz of his family coming from behind him slowly ebb as he forced more distance between himself and the faded memories of his father.

When John reached some ways away after a while of walking, he heard the church bell go off again. John pulled his coat tighter against his body, hunched over, and shoved his hands into the pockets. He didn't try to keep his shoes clean from the dirt as they were covered in dust, grass stains, and some mud. Once again, he became a shadow in the hills, his hat rising up before dipping back down past a grassy hill.

THE FIELD OF SIMPLICITY
James Eady, eleventh grade

The breeze in the night sky,
Colder than the days of summer
The smell of freshly made food
Lingering through the air. The field's
Lights, shining brighter than a firefly.

Sitting up in the stands, I
Reflect back, wondering how I
Got here.

I did horrible things in my past.
Stealing like a thief. Lying like the
Boy who cried wolf.

I'm lucky to be here, lucky to have
A second chance.

The fields fall silent and tense, suddenly
Fill with cheers from the crowd. It
Grows louder, the team scores after
Running as fast as a prey would from a hunter.

By the end of the night, the smell of food
Fades away, like day when night comes.
Lots of shouting from the excited team members.
The once empty walkways are filled with
Parents and friends.

ANGER
Elaina Farmer, eleventh grade

Anger is hot.

It is as red and
Bright as fire,
It is sharp glares
And thrown punches.

Anger is cold.

It is blue and
As biting as frost,
It is dead stares
And a sharp tongue.

Anger is destructive
And ever raging.

That is what I have learned,
What I have been told,
And what I have seen

I don't know Anger.
I have never felt its heat,
Or it's iciness.

I have never to felt its fists
Take mine
And hold them tight –
Or swing

What I describe as *anger*
Is *emptiness*;

It is that feeling you get
When thinking of an old friend –
One who left years ago
One who never stayed in contact.

You *know*
You are supposed to
Feel something
But there is *nothing*.

My anger is not black.
Or white.
It's gray.
That shade of gray that has no "opposite"

Sometimes, it is hot
Like a dry summer day
(never hotter)

Sometimes it is cold
Like a late fall night
(never colder)

My anger is not lashing out
Like red
Nor is it biding its time
Like blue

It is either
Ignoring, or
Accepting.

My anger
Is walking away
Not to plan
But to process.

And sometimes
I hate it
I don't fit in
Because of it

And I don't know
What others mean
When they talk about
Anger.

DREAM WALKING (EXCERPT FROM A LONGER WORK)

Tatum Alice Fineout, eleventh grade

I knew what was to come next. I gathered sentimental belongings and packed provisions. I slipped into slightly tattered clothes, threw on my comfiest boots, and ran out the back door to avoid meeting with the rioters. I made a run for the dock, almost tripping with every step. The closer I got to the sandy beach, the more the sand turned black. Reaching the docks, my eyes widened. Every ship was engulfed in bright orange flames. Looking back to the town I witnessed the mob lighting the town's bank in flames. The sight of these people destroying my beloved town was enough to bring tears to my eyes. I was frozen with fear and filled with the desire to stay. I looked back at the town, my home, burning to nothingness. The flames from the docks have spread to the surrounding vegetation, eating away the plants and trees. Now, with a face flushed and soaked with tears, running was the only option for me.

As soon as I felt my feet sink into Earth's soil, I knew I was close to my safe haven. The wind from the bay blew harshly in my eyes, blowing away the tears, and leaving my nose red as can be. The winds, though cold, felt warm to the touch; making me able to smile and able to relax. The sounds of the angry town faded, but the light of the fires were still visible, however distant. Removing my boots and setting my satchel down, I drifted slowly toward the water's edge. Having the cold, salt-saturated ocean cover my feet and brush my ankles gave me a kind chill. In this moment, I felt as if time was an illusion. I remembered my brother's supposed return from visiting with our father while my mind was clear; I hoped he would not return today after this horrible event.

I closed my eyes for a few minutes, taking in the feeling of safety the haven gave me, and holding it close and dear. I reminisced about the times I'd had with my brother, like the strudel incident on Christmas when our stone oven fed its flames into our hut. It made our whole kitchen catch fire, the burn marks still remain in the stone. Or the night our town got ambushed by donkeys on All Hallow's Eve. My brother and I let them loose and dressed them in lambs blood to prank the town's folk. I am very fond of remembering the past, however, I hate venturing too deep into it. I opened my eyes and looked to the horizon searching for the rising sun, but my vision went foggy.

I blinked and felt a piercing heat in my side; looking down at my side I saw the handle of a silver blade lodged below my ribs. I went to grasp the haft of my blade, but my blood trickled down my side and covered the tips of my fingers. My thoughts ran hazy, and my motions were heavy. I took many steps back before tripping over my feet, and fell into the stiff sand. Before slipping into unconsciousness I saw the man who had stabbed me get stabbed himself, but not by a dagger like he did to me.

He was stabbed with a sword. The wielder of the sword was blurry, but I could make out his boots. They were black leather; embroidered with the head of a gorgon and the wings of a phoenix. Behind him were many other pairs of boots in brown, black, pasty red, and some olive green. They all trampled around yelling profanities and slang; the last thing I heard was the voices of two people.

"He looks alive still, what should we do?"

"Bring him aboard with the others, Doc will fix 'im."

YOU'RE PERFECT THE WAY YOU ARE

Lillian Greenman, eleventh grade

Dear Mr. Pumpkin,

I can't help but ask, why are you so moldy?
Why do you leak maggots?
You're supposed to be glorious and plump.
What happened, Mr. Pumpkin?

Spiders climb along your skin, but you don't mind.
Your head is sunken in, Mr. Pumpkin! Isn't your brain smushed?
No worry passes your mind while you reek like puke.

Your pattern is weird, Mr. Pumpkin!
You're supposed to have round ridges along your body
But instead you have waffle imprints along your spine

Oh, Mr. Pumpkin, I do advise you to wash up
I want to see your bright orange scalp shine
Almost like a block of cheese does

What's that noise, Mr. Pumpkin? Do you hear that winning?
Oh it's you! You're molting tears, Mr. Pumpkin!
Oh, Mr. Pumpkin, don't cry!

You know what, I'm sorry
I am sorry for contradicting your appearance

You shimmer with beauty, Mr. Pumpkin!
From your matte orange peel of skin
To your sparkling guts fused with your glossy seeds
And your camo variation of colors

Oh, Mr. Pumpkin, you are glorious!
You don't reek!
When waffted your aroma is of sweetness
Almost like a warmed cinnamon stick on a cold evening

Now, Mr. Pumpkin, I can't help but tell you, your uniqueness is your
    beauty.
Hell, if we all looked the same there wouldn't be any appreciation for
    uniqueness
A world full of look-alikes would be atrocious!
Don't change anything about yourself, Mr. Pumpkin.
You're perfect.

FAMILY TIES
A PLAY
Brent Mankowski, eleventh grade

<u>Cast of Characters</u>

MICHAEL COATS
Twenty-two-year-old, loves his friends. Chill. Jokes a lot. Café worker. Very Smiley.
   (Costume: Headband with flowers on it, leather armless vest with tassels, yellow undershirt, jeans OR black pants, rugged brown Tennie shoes.)

CLIFF SKYE
Forty-three-year-old. Cold and un-reacting. Angry. Detective.
   (Costume: White dress shirt, Black pants, brown suspenders, black loafers.)

ANNABELLE HEIDE
Twenty-Three-year-old. easily angered. easily annoyed. Unemployed
(Costume: Yellow shirt, brown vest /w arms no tassels, white baggy pants, worn black Tennie shoes.)

<u>Scene</u>
Street, with some buildings in the background and a trash can.

<u>Time</u>
2023 – Summer – California

Scene 1

AT RISE; -No lights-
A street with MICHAEL on the left, his back against the wall. He has a bag of spray paint. To his left is ANNABELLE, standing next to MICHAEL. To his right, on the other side of the stage CLIFF was standing there, also holding his phone.

-Spotlight on MICHAEL and ANNABELLE-
MICHAEL grabs a bottle of spray paint turning to the wall as he looks at ANNABELLE, who also grabs a can, them both standing up to the wall.

MICHAEL
Jeez, it's been a while since we've done this, hasn't it?

ANNABELLE
Really? It's only been four days, dude. And even so, you usually wait a week or two so Cliff doesn't scold you for it.

> (MICHAEL and ANNABELLE start spraying the wall with only sound effects coming out. After a few seconds, they look at the cans together.)

>> MICHAEL
>> See? I told you it's been a while!

>> ANNABELLE
>> It hasn't been that long! (pause) I'll go get some more.

(ANNABELLE grabs the bag of spray paint as well as MICHAEL's can and walks off the stage to the left. Michael then picks his phone up like he's on a call. Stage lights shift over to CLIFF, focusing him with a spotlight.)

CLIFF

Hello? (pause) Yes. Is this Annabelle Heide? Who's asking? Cliff Skye. Look, I need to meet you on Western Avenue, I have some (pause) things I need to talk about with you. It's about your friend, Michael, He- (pause)

(CLIFF pulls his phone away from his face, staring at it as he sighs loudly.)

Well. She should be on her way then.

(CLIFF sighs as he puts his phone in his pocket, looking off to the side, then at the buildings next to him. Shortly after, ANNABELLE comes onto the stage, from the right. She walks up to CLIFF and grabs his collar. The lights on the stage light up the entire right side, still not lighting up MICHAEL.)

ANNABELLE

Just what kind of dirt do you have on Michael. I know you and I know your games, Cliff.

(CLIFF raises his hands in fear before slowly putting them down, realizing who it was. He then stares at her in the eyes.)

CLIFF

Putting your hands on a police officer? That's one way to go to jail, and for less to no reason.

(ANNABELLE scoffs as she lets go of him, taking a few steps back, but still in a scrappy body stance. CLIFF fixes his shirt as he looks at his shirt, then he looks back at ANNABELLE.)

ANNABELLE

Oh, shut up. Just what new method are you trying to get Michael kicked out of the city?

(CLIFF makes a small smile for a second before it fading. ANNABELLE still has a scowl on her face. MICHAEL would be on a phone call, still not ever facing the two. CLIFF pulls out a plastic baggy with photos in it, handing it to ANNABELLE.)

CLIFF

How about you take a look for yourself and tell me what you see.

(ANNABELLE snatches the bag out of CLIFF's hand, CLIFF not reacting to the sudden movement. ANNABELLE opens the bag and pulls some of the photos out, looking at them as her expression gets petrified more and more.)

ANNABELLE

Where did you get these? These... These shouldn't even exist.

CLIFF

I found them in two places. One, at Michael's parents' house, and the other online, I had to do a lot of digging tho--

(He's cut off by ANNABELLE.)

ANNABELLE

OK, so you just admitted to stalking, what the absolute hell, man?

CLIFF

That's, kinda what detectives such as myself do. Anyways, if you need any-more information on your "friend", you know where to find me.

(CLIFF walks away, past MICHAEL. MICHAEL looks up at CLIFF, but just stays out of view, backing off. ANNABELLE scoffs as she stares at him – not seeing MICHAEL. ANNA-BELLE grabs her phone out of her pocket, putting the photos back into the bag as she dials a number, then puts her phone up to her ear. The stage lights focus on MICHAEL and ANNA-BELLE. MICHAEL jumps a bit as his phone rings. He brings his phone up to his ear.)

MICHAEL
(Same time as ANNABELLE)
Hey best buddy, what's going on?

ANNABELLE
(Sametime as MICHAEL)
Has Cliff shown you what *YOU* did?

(MICHAEL backs up from his phone as he looks at his phone, then putting his ear back to it. ANNABELLE furiously paces around the street.)

MICHAEL
Whoa—Whoa slow down, what did you say?

ANNABELLE
Come to Western Avenue. Just. Hurry. Up.

(MICHAEL looks around towards the street signs.)

MICHAEL

Actually, I'm already on the street, where are you- Oh I see you!

(MICHAEL starts looking around, then sees ANNABELLE.
All stage lights come on. MICHAEL waves all happily, and
ANNABELLE starts just walking towards him. MICHAEL
then starts walking towards her as well.)

MICHAEL

Hey, Best buddy! What did Mr. Skye talk abo--

(ANNABELLE pushes the bag of photos into MICHAEL's chest. He
gets pushed back, he scoffs as he stares at the bag)

MICHAEL

What's this?

(MICHAEL opens it, pulling the photos out as he starts to
look through it as his eyes widen, his smile dissipating.)

ANNABELLE

Photos of your house, and you in it. Why haven't you ever told me your
family was part of a-

MICHAEL

I told you not to talk about my family. This. This shouldn't exist, at all.
Who gave you this?

(MICHAEL's expression drops to a blank look. ANNA-
BELLE backs up a bit from him as he keeps going through the
photos, eventually crumpling them in his hand.)

ANNABELLE

F-From Cliff. He just asked me to meet him a--

(ANNABELLE starts getting nervous, disliking when
MICHAEL gets upset like this. MICHAEL takes a step for-
wards in her direction, getting closer to her.)

MICHAEL

And why did you agree to meet him?

MICHAEL
(Same time as ANNABELLE.)

What is wrong with you? You know he just wants to kick me out of this
town.

ANNABELLE
(Same time as MICHAEL.)

I didn't- He just asked and It sounded like it was harmful towards you--

(MICHAEL keeps pushing himself towards ANNABELLE as
he scowls. ANNABELLE eventually pushes him in the chest,
causing him to back up into a trash can, which he kicks over by
accident, knocking trash out of it.)

ANNABELLE

DUDE, BACK OFF.

(ANNABELLE breathes heavily, leaned over due to strain
on her mind. MICHAEL stares at her as he clears his throat,
brushing himself off as he looks at her.)

MICHAEL

S-Sorry. You know it's a sensitive topic.

ANNABELLE

Yeah. Yeah, sorry. I know your Family is a really sensitive topic.

(Silence ensues with MICHAEL and ANNABELLE look around before MICHAEL sighs, turning away from ANNABELLE)

MICHAEL

Call Cliff and get him over here. It's been three years of him trying to kick me out of this town, and it's time we end this.

(MICHAEL rips the entire bag up, dropping it as he crosses his arms. He scoffs as he looks away. ANNABELLE nods as she gulps, grabbing her phone and tapping a few buttons before putting it to her ear.)

(MICHAEL and ANNABELLE start mouthing words as the lights go dark, then they walk off to the left of the stage. CLIFF walks on from the right of the stage, walking with his hands in his pockets. CLIFF stops in the middle of the stage and grabs his phone, which is vibrating. He puts it up to his ear before MICHAEL runs back on stage from the right, pushing CLIFF from the back, making him stumble to the ground, falling and cracking his phone, glass shattering. ANNABELLE quickly runs up behind MICHAEL, staying behind him.)

MICHAEL

WHAT. DID YOU DO.

(CLIFF is startled, backing up from the enraged MICHAEL, CLIFF Gets to his feet quickly, putting his 'dukes' up.)

CLIFF

WHOA WHOA. NEUKEN. DON'T--

MICHAEL

NO. You're gonna shut up and tell me how you found those-

ANNABELLE

Michael. Calm. Down.

(MICHAEL sighs as he backs up, standing next to ANNA-
BELLE as CLIFF relaxes, still with his hands a bit raised.)

CLIFF

Now. What do you want? And what are you doing, putting your hands
on an off--

MICHAEL

Oh, cut it with that officers bologna. I'm here because you have private
photos of my past.

(CLIFF smiles, and relaxes, crossing his arms.)

CLIFF

Ah. So that's why you've come. Well MICHAEL, if you don't want those
to become publi--

MICHAEL

If you even so much as share that with someone else other then Annabelle,
I'll--

CLIFF

WOULD YOU STOP, (pause) cutting me off. Now, as I was saying. If you don't want those photos to become public, just leave. Leave this town and take your misdemeanor elsewhere.

(A moment of silence as MICHAEL and ANNABELLE Look at each other, they look mad. They look back at CLIFF.)

MICHAEL
(Same time as ANNABELLE)
Stop trying to get me out of this stupid town.

ANNABELLE
(Same time as MICHAEL)
Stop trying to get Michael out of this town, dude.

(MICHAEL and ANNABELLE look at each other, then back.)

CLIFF

Well, if he didn't spray paint every free wall he sees he'd be fine, or if he didn't break into people's houses whenever they say something mean about him or his friend, he'd be fine, but no.

MICHAEL

And that caused you to look for photos of my family, of that cursed house-hold. That cult of Satan? That name that made ME do those things in the photos that you found? I'll end your sad pathetic li---

(ANNABELLE stops MICHAEL's rant by covering his mouth.)

ANNABELLE

That's enough of your rant, Michael. Just. Cliff, why did you have to bring those up? You really wanna shun Michael out of the village like some sort of 1700's witch trial?

(CLIFF looks away, at the ground, then turns his back to the two, avoiding eye contact)

CLIFF

Whatever gets him out of my tow--

MICHAEL

OKAY, WHAT? No, I know me being a criminal isn't the only reason you want me out of here so WHY ARE YOU TRYING SO HA--

CLIFF

Your father made a deal with me, and he broke the promise.

(MICHAEL stops yelling, and backs up a bit, scoffing he stares at CLIFF's back.)

MICHAEL

(Monotone voice)

What type of deal.

(CLIFF turns back to MICHAEL as he scoffs.)

CLIFF

That, is none of your business. Just know things went south and you're the main reason that it got ruined. So now, I want to ruin you.

ANNABELLE

Revenge plot, huh? That's kinda a jerk move. And what did his dad even do?

MICHAEL

What didn't he do is the better question.

(MICHAEL and CLIFF both cross their arms. ANNA-BELLE looks at the two as she sighs.)

ANNABELLE

Okay, so he was a jerk, got it.

CLIFF

Not only that, but he made deals that he never held up. He was a part of multiple crime syndicates. As well-

MICHAEL

Shut up.

CLIFF

What?

(MICHAEL walks up to CLIFF, grabbing his collar as he pulls him a inch away from his face.)

MICHAEL

First of all stop talking with me and Annabelle like we're fine, because we're not. Second, if you ever talk about my family to anyone again, especially in front of me, I'm gonna make sure you don't talk again.

(MICHAEL stares down at CLIFF, dropping him as he turns his back to CLIFF, walking away.)

CLIFF

Then leave.

(MICHAEL pivots, turning around as he stares at CLIFF. CLIFF stares back as he backs up a little bit, looking away discouraged.)

Okay, fine, I won't show anyone. But if you continue to 'tag' walls and stuff, I'm gonna be forced to arrest you, and the news stories will be all over you. So-

MICHAEL

Yeah, Yeah, I know you'll be questioned and whatever. I'll stay out of trouble or whatever.

(CLIFF sighs as he shakes his head, turning away and going off stage to the left. MICHAEL looks back at ANNABELLE as he smiles. They both walk off the right.)

(The stage lights go dim and silence. Stage lights come on again, MICHAEL and ANNABELLE run on from the left.)

ANNABELLE

So, what are you gonna do?

MICHAEL

Me? What am I going to do? Nothing! Mr. Sky e always says she's going to do stuff yet he never does, and are you joking? Annabelle, when have I ever been caught?

ANNABELLE

Uh. Never, but that doesn't mean you'll always be able to avoid the cops. Also why do you call Cliff, Mr. Skye? And, what happened with your family? It sounded pretty drastic... Wait... never mind—Sorry.

MICHAEL

I call Mr. Skye that because that's what we're supposed to call him. And, eh I'll always find a way... and for that last question, it's just some family ties.

THE END

A NEW PRODUCTION
Randale McCuien, twelfth grade

On the grounds below orange and yellow leaves rest
Having completed their task

And finally rid of their strong green
Wearing new shades

The leaves move ever so slightly
Shifting either from gentle winds

 Or by little black peppered specks moving in unison.
Where to, I couldn't tell you,

But I do know they are good at their job.
Birds sing in harmonies, disharmonies, and otheries

Like a sucky middle school choir with a single star student
Small spotlights beam through the spots left by veteran leaves

True performers now join the pit, or, well, the ground.
My breath acts as a fog machine for the little play put on by the woods.

The fog weakens and my breath stills.
The light bends and I lose track of the little specks.
Not sure what color those leaves are.
They should be orange, yellow, or vermilion.
But everything looks a little blueish
What a fine production

I should probably stop hanging upside down from this tree.
Apt. 204
Lucas McSwain, twelfth grade

Looking around me I would stare
At the empty rooms
In such a small apartment,
That seemed so massive.

The only color visible,
A dull white.
I laid my blanket and pillow on the floor
And tucked myself in.

Above me was the popcorn ceiling,
I heard muffled yelling between a couple
From the wall left to me.

I stood up
Stared down out the window,
Squinting to see the dark parking lot.
A man with a scraggly beard
 Slumped next to the door
With a six-pack next to him.

I turned back and returned to my floor bed,
Thinking how this will be my home.
Nodding off
My head tilts back.

I opened my eyes,
Looking around me
And the sun glared at my eyes from the window.
I got up and walked outside,
Looking straight forward there was a small brown creek.
The glittering water flowed between the trees
So, I walked over and sat next to it.
A ruffling between branches beneath me,
Something flung beside my leg.

I look over by the tree on the right of me
Where the flash came from.
And saw,
A kid my age
Playing catch and release with toads.

Looking back,
Life wasn't always so bad.

MISS MIRROR
A PLAY
Dominic Montoya-Arlt, twelfth grade

<u>Cast of Characters</u>
RONNIE   Full first name is Veronica. In their late teens. Has issues with gender dysphoria. Prefers to dress in a traditionally masculine way because they are secretly a transgender man. Wears a plain button-up shirt, dress pants, and belt.

ANDREW   RONNIE's older brother, mid-twenties. A little oblivious at times. Loves RONNIE. RONNIE's legal guardian.

MISS MIRROR   A physical representation of RONNIE's psychological issues with their gender and the dissatisfaction resulting from it. Manifests as RONNIE's reflection, so she wears the same clothes RONNIE wears and mimics RONNIE's every movement. Wears too much makeup.

<u>Scene</u>

RONNIE's living room.

<u>Time</u>

Present.

<u>Scene</u>

AT RISE   Scene begins in the LIVING ROOM. A couch runs parallel to the back wall. A full-length "mirror" (an empty frame) stands stage left.

ANDREW enters stage right, holding out a suit jacket on a hanger. RONNIE follows a moment later.

RONNIE

You don't even wear it anymore! Just let me use it.

ANDREW

No, it's mine. Why don't you wear that dress Mom got you?

RONNIE

It's too revealing and I *despise* that shade of green.

ANDREW

No, not the green one. The blue one.

RONNIE

The blue one is even worse!

ANDREW

(increasingly exasperated) Then why did you wear it to the wedding?

RONNIE

I didn't know how horrible it was until I put it on and by then we were already almost late.

ANDREW

Why do you even want a jacket? You look okay as it is.

RONNIE

It might get cold.

ANDREW

It's summer.

RONNIE

It might get cold.

ANDREW

Just put on a sweater.

RONNIE

Do you think literally anyone would put on a sweater for prom? I need that jacket. It's basically mine anyway.

ANDREW

What?

RONNIE

I wear it all the time. It's basically mine.

ANDREW

You're really not helping your case right now. Last I checked, it doesn't say "Veronica"-

RONNIE

(Interrupting) -Ronnie-

ANDREW

-on the tag, it says "Andrew".

RONNIE

If you don't let me use it tonight, I just won't go.

ANDREW

You wouldn't. You're graduating this year. You wouldn't miss this. (beat) Why do you wear it all the time?

RONNIE

I like it. It makes me feel better.

ANDREW

Do you need your anxiety meds?

RONNIE

No, not like that. (softly) It feels... right. When I look in a mirror, I like who's looking back.

ANDREW

Oh. Is it like an anxiety thing or...?

RONNIE

It's nothing. I can go like this.

ANDREW

No, here.

RONNIE

Are you sure?

(Andrew nods.)

Thank you.

ANDREW

I'll be waiting in the car. You go do makeup or whatever it is you do.

(ANDREW exits. RONNIE sighs and puts the jacket on. They turn to the mirror to check themself. MISS MIRROR steps into the mirror frame. She will reflect any movements RONNIE makes. RONNIE turns to look at herself at different angles. Suddenly, MISS MIRROR speaks. This is not the first time RONNIE has encountered MISS MIRROR.)

MISS MIRROR

(Cheery) Hello!

RONNIE

(Resigned) Oh god.

MISS MIRROR

You know, I was listening to your conversation earlier. Those dresses aren't revealing, Veronica. You just don't want to be seen. Society thanks you for finally realizing how much of a stain you are.

RONNIE

The only stain I see is the one looking back at me. Now buzz off. Go wherever it is you usually go.

MISS MIRROR

(Sarcastic) Oh, is this a bad time for you? I guess I'll just stop being your reflection-

RONNIE

Stop it. You're not a reflection. If you really were a reflection, other people would see you. And hear you talk.

MISS MIRROR

Do you think I want to be *your* reflection? Do you think I want to look like old skin nailed to a piece of wood?

RONNIE

Ironic, coming from a literal mirror creature.

MISS MIRROR

Maybe if you wore more make-up, you could hide your craterface. Oh, but you gave up on make-up years ago...

(RONNIE takes a tie from the drawer and begins to tie a Windsor knot. MISS MIRROR takes out the same tie and also begins to tie in sync.)

RONNIE

Make-up is for those who can waste time on it.

MISS MIRROR

Those people care, Veronica. They want people to see the best face they have. No, you gave up on make-up because you never did any of it right.

RONNIE

Yeah? And what's the right way, *Miss Mirror*?

MISS MIRROR

Well, there's only wrong ways with you. Everything on your face is a 'Dead-End' sign in larvae form.

RONNIE

And yet people still like me.

(MISS MIRROR laughs.)

MISS MIRROR

O-kay. Need I remind you? You have no friends. Your brother barely puts up with you, and only because your dead mom told him to.

(RONNIE pauses tying her tie. MISS MIRROR stops in sync.)

RONNIE

Shut up. That's... that's not true.

(RONNIE resumes tying, as does MISS MIRROR.)

MISS MIRROR

Sorry, honey, but someone needs to break it to you, and I'm the only someone you ever talk to.

RONNIE

I talk to Andrew all of the time.

MISS MIRROR

He doesn't even know you. You don't even know you.

RONNIE

I know who I am.

MISS MIRROR

Yeah? Who?

RONNIE

Shut up.

(RONNIE finishes tying a tie; it looks like a mess. MISS MIRROR mimics.)

MISS MIRROR

Oh, and now look what you've done. You can't even manage a tie.

(RONNIE yanks the tie off, lets it fall to the ground, and runs her fingers through her hair. After a moment, she peels off the jacket and tosses it on the couch. ANDREW pokes his head in.)

ANDREW

HEY! WE NEED TO- Oh, dear. Let me help.

(ANDREW picks up the jacket from the couch.)

RONNIE

No, I-

ANDREW

You should put it on.

(ANDREW hands her the jacket.)

MISS MIRROR

You really need help for this? You're pathetic.

RONNIE

Andy, it's not-

ANDREW

Come on, you said you wanted to wear it. This is not something you want to miss.

RONNIE

(angry) You don't think I know that?

(RONNIE reluctantly puts on the jacket.)

MISS MIRROR

Oh, so snappy! Is it that time of the month, honey?

RONNIE

Shut up.

ANDREW

I didn't even say anything!

RONNIE

Sorry, I'm just nervous.

ANDREW

Are you sure you don't want your meds?

MISS MIRROR

Oh, meds aren't what she needs. She needs some good, strong rope.

(RONNIE visibly tenses. ANDREW straightens RONNIE's jacket.)

ANDREW

Are you okay? You look like you're about to throw up.

RONNIE

I'll be okay.

(ANDREW dusts off the coat.)

MISS MIRROR

Why don't you tell him? Why don't you tell him that last week, you went to the pharmacy and bought enough bleach to fill a bucket? Why don't you tell him that the only way you'll ever fix your body is if you stop living in it? Why don't you tell him that the only reason you haven't done it yet is because you don't want to put him in debt for the funeral? (ANDREW takes a step back, looks RONNIE up and down.)

ANDREW

There we go. That look good to you?

(RONNIE begins to cry. MISS MIRROR begins to laugh.)

RONNIE

I'm sorry. I'm so sorry. I'm so sorry. I... can't...

(ANDREW hugs RONNIE.)

ANDREW

It's okay. Shh, shh. It's alright. If you want, we can stay.

RONNIE

(Sobbing) It's not that. You don't know. How could you know?

ANDREW

Tell me. I'll listen.

MISS MIRROR

And what will he think? How bad will he take it?

ANDREW

I know we're not that close, but I care about you. You've always been there.

MISS MIRROR

And how will that change once he finds out you don't feel like a woman? That you're thinking these wrong, stupid thoughts?

ANDREW

Come on, sit down.

(ANDREW leads RONNIE to the couch, where they sit. MISS MIRROR exits as RONNIE steps away from the mirror.)

ANDREW

You know, I remember when you were born. I had been taken to the hospital to see Mom. She was so tired, she couldn't even keep her eyes open.

(RONNIE begins to calm down taking deep breaths.)

She looked at me, and she said, "I want you to know that even though I'll be spending so much time with your sister, it doesn't mean I don't love you. She loves you, too. You'll see it when she wakes up. And you better love her, too. No matter what." And I looked at you, all curled up and red in the face, and I looked at Mom, and I said, "She's so small, she can fit in my heart just fine." (beat) And you haven't left.

(RONNIE breathes deep. The sobbing has subsided.)

RONNIE

I- I hate my body. Every time I look in the mirror, I feel a knot in my throat. I hate my chest. I hate dresses, and heels, and anything like that. I'm not- I'm a man. I'm a *man*.

(There is a pause. ANDREW is taken aback; for him this is out of left field. RONNIE is tense, waiting.)

ANDREW

Oh. I see. Oh dear. Yeah. That's...

(ANDREW stands up and takes a step away.)

I think...(long pause) I think that jacket suits you. You just need the tie.

(ANDREW picks up the tie and loops it over RONNIE's neck. Then ANDREW pulls RONNIE to his feet.)

ANDREW

So, you start out uneven, one end way lower than the other. Then...

(ANDREW begins to slowly tie a Windsor knot with the tie, showing RONNIE how to tie a tie. RONNIE is still sniffling.)

You loop it around like this, and then like this again. And then, you pull it up through the middle and there you go. I've always been better at doing this on other people than me.

(ANDREW finishes the tie and closes off the jacket.)

RONNIE

Thank you.

ANDREW

Why don't you check to make sure it looks right?

(RONNIE approaches the mirror hesitantly. There is a conspicuous lack of MISS MIRROR. RONNIE takes in his reflection in full. He smiles for the first time in the play and turns around to face ANDREW.)

RONNIE

Thank you.

ANDREW

Mom would've loved to see you like this. (Beat) Now come on, we've got to go or we're going to be late.

(ANDREW bustles off to exit. RONNIE looks at the mirror again and exits.)

SCENE END

BREAK A LEG
A PLAY
Mason Moran, twelfth grade

<u>Cast of Characters</u>

SAM   Male. Seventeen years old. Not a dance student. In love with DAVID.

DAVID   Male. Eighteen years old. He's the best dancer in dance class and knows it. Wears all black.

BREANNA   Female. Seventeen years old. SAM's best friend.

NURSE   A nurse in a walk-in clinic.

<u>Scene</u>

A dance studio. A walk-in clinic.

<u>Time</u>

Present.

Scene 1

AT RISE: The right side of the stage is the main room of the dance studio. On the left side is a hallway with a waiting bench. A door separates the two.

DAVID is practicing in the main room.

Lights up on the hallway.

SAM is pacing.

BREANNA is sitting on the bench

BREANNA
Are you going in there or what?

SAM
Just gimme a second. Don't rush me.

BREANNA
You've talked with him before. What's so different about now?

SAM
Yeah for like a second!
            (A beat.)
What do you think he'll say?

BREANNA
He'll probably just laugh. Or say something a human being would say. Look I think you're stressing about this too hard.

SAM
Are you kidding me! This is like the make or break of my life! God, he's so perfect. If I even so much as stutter, I'll ruin his aura.

BREANNA
What?

SAM
Oh, he's out of my league, isn't he? There's no way I could be with-

BREANNA
(Standing up, grabbing SAMs shoulders.)
Oh, get a hold of yourself!

SAM
Wha-

BREANNA
Look, man. If I learned anything from my ex it's that persistence is key. If you want him, and he's out of your league, you've gotta earn him.

SAM
Persistence?

BREANNA
Yes. He may seem scary but I'm sure he has a weak spot. I mean you remember why you joined the dance club in the first place, right?

SAM
Right.

BREANNA
Oh! Here take these.
(BREANNA gives SAM several note cards. SAM begins to study them.)

SAM
Bree, these are terrible. How did you even come up with these?

BREANNA
Oh, I just found them online.

                        SAM

Man, I don't know-

                        BREANNA

            (BREANNA starts pushing SAM toward the door. At the
            same time as SAM.)
Alright buster, get in there!

                        SAM

            (At the same time as BREANNA.)
Wait! Wait! Wait!
            (SAM gets pushed through the door and into the main room.
            Lights up on the main room. To BREANNA.)

Hey! Quit pushing me!
            (SAM spots DAVID and freezes. A beat. SAM approaches
            DAVID.)
U-uh, h-hey.
            (DAVID doesn't appear to notice him. SAM holds up one of
            the note cards in front of himself. Reading the card.)
Ahem. Are you religious, because I think dancing with me could be the
answer to your prayers.

                        DAVID

I'm not religious.

                        SAM

Oh, heh heh. Yeah... I'm Sam.
            (SAM reaches for a handshake. DAVID doesn't take it.)

                        DAVID

David.

                            SAM

Yeah... I think we met at the audition?

                            DAVID

Don't recall.

                            SAM

Oh, well, hey I was wondering if... I could dance with you?

                            DAVID

Sorry, but as you can see I'm in the middle of polishing my routine

                            SAM

Oh, well I'd really like to learn it. And there were these guys in the hallway.
They said you oozed confi-dance.

                            DAVID

Good for them.

                            SAM

Here, let me...
             (SAM attempts to match DAVID's dancing.)

                            DAVID

You're doing it wrong.

                            SAM

So? I want to dance, so I'm gonna dance.

                            DAVID

Whatever. Do as you wish.

             (They both dance for a beat. SAM stops dancing.)

                                SAM

oh!

> (SAM looks at another card and then holds his breath for ten
> seconds before exhaling. Looking back at the note.)

Hey! You almost killed me! I thought of dancing with you and forgot how
to breathe.

> (Beat.)

What?

> (Neither of them looking, DAVID dances into SAM, toppling
> both. SAM falls onto DAVIDs leg. A loud crunching noise can
> be heard. DAVID shrieks in pain.)

                                SAM

Oh my god! Are you alright?

> (DAVID is writhing and groaning with pain. BREANNA
> enters.)

                             BREANNA

Oh my god, what happened!

                                SAM

I didn't mean to!

                             BREANNA

When I told you to find his weak spot, I meant emotionally.

> (DAVID inhales sharply in pain.)

SAM
> (To BREANNA.)

Oh, just shut it. Go get help.

BREANNA
(While exiting.)
What am I, your servant?

DAVID

Why did you get in my way?

SAM

I'm so sorry! I didn't mean to run into you, really I didn't.

(pause, David holds his leg in pain)

Here, let me see...
(DAVID groans in agony. SAM rolls up DAVIDS pant leg. DAVID shoves SAM.)

DAVID

Don't touch me!

SAM

OW! What the heck, man, that hurt!
(SAM holds his shoulder.)

DAVID

Are you kidding me? You just broke my leg!

SAM

I was just trying to help you!

(BREANNA bursts through the door, walking toward DAVID.)

                    BREANNA
Alright, my mom's here. Help me pick him up.

                       SAM
What? I thought I told you to call for help.

                    BREANNA
Yeah, I did.

                       SAM
Like, an ambulance kind of help.

                    BREANNA
Oh please, he can't be that hurt. We're just gonna take him to the clinic.

        (DAVID groans in agony.)

                       SAM
Whatever. Help me will you?
        (SAM stands up.)
You take that side. I'll take this side.

                      DAVID
        (SAM and BREANNA grab DAVID.)
OW! That's my bad leg idiot!
        (BREANNA lets go of one leg and repositions.)

                    BREANNA
Sorry.

        (SAM and BREANNA begin to lift DAVID up and start
        walking for the door.)

BREANNA

(At the same time as SAM.)

Okay this way. Oop. Okay this way. Keep going. Alright now, pivot. Geez, you're heavy. Ok, just a little more.

SAM

(Same time as BREANNA.)

Yup, okay. Okay. And this way. Alright. Hold on a second. Okay, I'm good. Alright and this way. Alright.

DAVID

OW!

SAM & BREANNA

Sorry!

(SAM, BREANNA, and DAVID exit.)

(BLACKOUT)

Scene 2

AT RISE: A clinic. A hospital gurney sits on the left side of the stage. A table sits next to the gurney. The right side is the waiting room with a few chairs and a flower pot lined up against the wall.

DAVID is lying on the gurney.

A NURSE can be seen bandaging DAVIDs leg.

SAM and BREANNA sit in the waiting room.

Lights up on the waiting room.

BREANNA

So, what happened?

SAM

He danced into me.

BREANNA

Ah.

SAM

(SAM stands up to leave.)
Welp, I guess I'll get going.

BREANNA

Wait! Aren't you gonna apologize? Finish the mission?

SAM

What do you think he'll say? "Oh, don't worry about it, I understand."
Besides, I'm not even sure if I want him now.

BREANNA

What do you mean?

SAM

He pushed me...

BREANNA

You sound like a child.

(SAM begins to leave. BREANNA stands up.)
Wait! At least apologize to him.

SAM

(SAM stops.)

Why do you care?

BREANNA

Why do I care? Cause I'm your friend... and cause I messed up with my ex

SAM

Your ex? What does he have to do with any of this?

BREANNA

Sam, I went through this same thing with my ex.

SAM

You broke his leg?

BREANNA

No, I mean the whole giving up thing. I thought he was out of my league, that I wasn't meant for him. I haven't stopped thinking about him since.
    (Beat.)
If you leave him now you'll regret it when you're off looking for some other guy. If I were you... which I was, I would at least talk to him while it's still up in the air. Even if it doesn't work out at least it'll be official.

    (BREANNA sits down. SAM takes a deep breath and starts heading for the door to the hospital room.)
Ooh!
    (BREANNA takes a flower out of a nearby flower pot and hands it to DAVID.)
Good luck.
    (DAVID takes it and enters the E.R. Lights up on E.R.)

DAVID

What are you doing here?

SAM

Coming to see if you're okay.

DAVID

I'm just peachy.

SAM

Well, that's good.

(SAM begins to leave but is blocked by BREANNA at the door. SAM turns back to DAVID.)

Why did you shove me?

DAVID

Excuse me?

SAM

I was just trying to check your foot.

DAVID

What are you talking about?

SAM

Remember? I tried to check your foot, and you shoved me to the ground. It really hurt.

DAVID

Well, even if I did do that, you broke my leg!

                                SAM

I didn't mean to, ok! I was just trying to... talk to you.

                               DAVID

I don't need your excuses. Get out of here before I break YOUR leg.

                                SAM
                  (SAM throws the flower to the ground.)
God, why are you so mean! And to think I was gonna ask you out.
                       (SAM covers his mouth.)

                               DAVID

What.

                                SAM

I-I, um...

                               DAVID
                            (Surprised.)
Wait, you were hitting on me?

                                SAM

You're only just now realizing this?

                               DAVID

Wait, but that doesn't make any sense. So, you're not with those other
guys?

                                SAM

What other guys.

                               DAVID

Wow, you're stupid. Confi-dance?

SAM

Hey!

DAVID

Well, no, Wait I didn't mean it like that... I'm sorry, I just... I thought you were messing with me.

SAM

What?

DAVID

The old dance captain's been sending his posse to mess with me all week. I guess he's not a fan of me stealing the title. I've tried to ignore them so far, but they're really hard to ignore. Look, I'm sorry.

SAM

What? No, I'm the one who should be apologizing. I'm the one who stopped dancing. I interrupted your routine. I never even wanted to be a dancer. That's why I joined the club. I wanted to be with you-

DAVID
                (Cutting SAM off.)
Look, it's fine, alright? How about I buy you lunch someday and we call it even?

SAM

Oh! Uh... sure!
                (beat.)
Welp... see you later.
                (SAM picks the flower off the ground and rests it on the table
                next to the gurney)
Here.

(SAM heads for the door, but stops just before it. SAM fist pumps the air, whispering.)

Yes.

END PLAY

MY SEAHORSE
Ella Mullens, eleventh grade

That pretty necklace wasn't so pretty. Its metal was silver and cold, though turned rusted over time. The metal was intricately woven and molded into a bunch of spiny, sharp tendrils, like miniature tentacles. The little pieces formed the shape of a majestic, abstract seahorse. I adore seahorses—they're so cute and simple. My seahorse was hollow, and she hung on a thin metal chain. Inside of her was a small pearl. A real pearl, picked off a real beach, on the coast of a real ocean, down in Florida. Or at least, that's what the card said. The pearl was tiny and white, almost iridescent in the right sunshine. It rattled around inside my seahorse with every step I took, as she rose and fell against my chest, matching my stride as her cold chain was warmed by the back of my neck. The chain practically molded itself into my skin, for I never took it off. Not at the doctor's, not in the shower, not in the pool, and not in bed. Her bright, blindingly silver body grew dark and chipped from constant wear.

I didn't get my seahorse in some cool, emotional way. She was given to me by a completely insignificant person in a completely insignificant way. He was a boy, and he stood tall and lanky. His skin was pale from a lack of Vitamin D. His hair was long, because I liked long hair. Despite my begging, he never washed it. It always hung in loose, greasy strands in front of his eyes, but on the rare occasions it was washed, it was a fluffy brown cloud of heaven that I loved running my fingers through. His eyes were a dark blue, darker than mine, but so similar. I rarely saw those eyes: they were either covered by the greasy strands, or they were looking at something that wasn't me.

Most people tell me not to think about him. They tell me to throw away his gifts and the memories with them. I've tried to do that, but here I am, writing about those very gifts that I threw away. Back when I first got my seahorse, I was so happy. I let that silly little gift block out all the warning signs. He bought me a pretty necklace—surely he loved me? He bought it while he was in Florida, on a family vacation. He said he got it at a small shack just off the beach to the ocean. The pearl was supposedly picked from that very beach, and specially placed into the hand-crafted metal seahorse. The boy that bought it for me told me it was very expensive, and told me I should be grateful, for no one else but him had a kind enough heart to spend money on a girl like me. So of course, I was eternally grateful. That little seahorse followed me everywhere I went. She was with me through the good times, the bad times, the empty times. Sometimes I wish I still had her, until I remember how I met her.

Now that I think about it, my seahorse wasn't all that great. I thought she was my best friend, but really, she lied to me. She let me believe that the boy that bought her for me could do no harm. *If he was willing to spend so much money on a little piece of jewelry, just for me, then he must not mean it when he calls me ugly*, I would think. When he called me worthless, pathetic, all the names he knew I hated. When he pushed me around, controlled me, lied to me. None of that bothered me, not so long as I had my seahorse hanging around my neck. Little did I know, there were other girls who got even better necklaces than me. Necklaces of pearls, gold, diamonds. But they didn't care about their necklaces as much as I did. They took their necklaces off when they weren't trying to impress. I never took mine off.

Sometimes, when I miss my seahorse, I think back to the moment I met her. It was at school, which is normally such a hollow and draining place. But I was sitting against that cold brick wall, next to that boy, because I couldn't sit with anyone else. He handed me a small blue box, and I was confused, and I objected, because I didn't want him to spend money on me. I didn't want him to go broke, even though I knew he spent way more money on other girls who only cared about gifts. He insisted I take the blue box, and so I did. When I opened it, I was so excited to see that seahorse. That boy never remembered things about me—he even forgot my birthday. Twice. I imagine all the birthdays of all the girlfriends got mixed up. But he remembered something about *me*: that I love seahorses. He recalled that little detail about me, and nobody else. No one ever remembered details about me, especially not him. It made me so happy.

I immediately hung my seahorse around my neck, and I vowed then and there to never take her off.

Thinking back to the two years that I wore that seahorse religiously, it's kind of bittersweet. I kept her for a little while after the breakup—I thought she was like a trophy, and she represented how strong I was to make it through. But I realized that was just an excuse. My seahorse, though I loved her so much for so long, was my enemy all along. Through every argument, I forgave that boy, and only because my seahorse told me to. My seahorse told me he loved me, even though he didn't. My seahorse came disguised to me as a token of unconditional love, despite setbacks. But that's not what she was. She was a liar, she was a devil hiding in the form of a little silver pendant. How could I keep her after all she did to me? So I threw her away. I held her in my palm, and I cried on her, my tears soaking into her little pearl, tainting its pure white color. When I was done, I threw her in my trash, I threw that trash in a plastic bag, I threw that plastic bag in the garbage bin, and I watched on Wednesday morning when the trash man showed up and dumped our bin into the back of his massive truck, and then drove off. As I watched him drive out of sight, I realized my seahorse was now gone forever. She's sitting somewhere, lost in a dump, buried under other trash that people don't care about. She's long gone, and so is the boy that gave her to me. So I find myself wondering, why am I still writing about them?

MY HUMBLE ABODE
Isabelle Plamondon, eleventh grade

There's a pasture by my grandparents' house,
a pasture filled with herds of cows.
The cows stampede down the dirt hills
into the pasture once the sun hits the glossy green of the leaves on the
    trees.
All you can hear is the jingling of the bells around the heifers' necks as
    they graze.

And by this pasture is a wild raspberry patch,
hidden in the tall bluegrass and rye.
We'd fill the bushel baskets with the sweet red berries
that always caught our eyes.

And by the raspberry patch are the gardens,
the gardens that are just out of reach for the pigs.
They always throw their squealing fits when you went out to harvest,
but the gardens have nothing left to offer.
It's early September and harvest is done.

And by the gardens and the pig pen are scattered bushes of blackberries,
None yet ripe enough to pick
And always rather prickly,
So much so that they'd get you if you weren't careful.

And in the middle of it all, is the big round bales of hay that I could
    never quite see over.
They'd loom like a mountain waiting to be climbed,
like a challenge waiting to be completed.
So we'd climb them with our bushel baskets and hearts full of
    anticipation.

These great big scratchy bales of hay could be quite difficult.
You'd put the bushel basket on the top,
find one of the bright orange strings that hold the bale together,
kick a foothold in the side of the bale, and climb your way using all your
    strength.
The dogs always jumped up with ease taunting us,
trying to get at the sweet red anticipation in the baskets.

Once you've completed the challenge and climbed the mountain,
you have the perfect view of the cow pasture and everything around you:
the pigs and the gardens,
the red raspberries and the green blackberries too young for picking,
 and the dogs in the fields of bluegrass and rye.

And the sounds,
Oh, the sounds!
The sound of wild grasses blowing with the breeze and the leaves,
the birds feasting on what's left of the raspberries,
the dogs playing about,
the muffled squeals and oinks of the pigs,
the bells on the cows as they graze,
as well as Grandma calling for dinner,

but this is not the place I call home.

After dinner is when we depart.
We pack up our things and go back to the start.
We travel on back to where we relax,
where a half acre is more than enough for us.
Where it always smells like a vanilla candle is lit,
where the birds and the bees all have their own niche.

Where our three dogs play all day,
where the button quail call each other from farther away.
Where the chickens are always rambunctious as I,
free-ranging about without a doubt,
and the rooster is always singing his tune
to the lovely ladies in our zoo.

Where I find the most peace,
in the chaos I like to call our hobby farm.

THE DEVIL
Vincent Redman, twelfth grade

The Devil is my friend
When I am alone, It is there
We gossip and plan
Talk future and past
When I am feeling down
It lulls me to bed

I take the offer graciously, but
As soon as I lie down
The Devil reminds me of what others say
You'll end up just like your psycho mother,
Said father.
She dresses like a slut,
Said grandmother,
Who helped me pick these very clothes.
You'll never be valued, and never loved,
Whispered the Devil
With whom I share all my thoughts.

The Devil and I had a fight
For power over my mind
The Devil has already won my body
I am stagnant
Not because I want to be
It fills my bones with lead
My mind with clouds

You've lost weight,
Said mother
Who looked prideful of my appearance
I have not eaten
Instead, the Devil
Eats me

POLARIZED POSTING: HOW INTERNET ALGORITHMS MAY BE PUSHING EXTREMIST IDEAS

Madeline Rowney, twelfth grade

There is no denying the horrific increase in mass shootings in the United States over the last twenty years. Between January 1st and April 17th of 2023, there were 163 violent crimes that fell under the umbrella of a mass shooting, according to ABC News. April 17th is only the 107th day of the year. Beyond the shootings themselves, the spike in extremist-related violence also cannot be ignored. From 2010-2020 there were 21 shootings linked with extremist ideology, leaving 164 people dead. Many officials, such as politicians and teachers, have pointed to social media as the culprit for these tragedies, bias-fueled Facebook feeds and toxic Instagram explore pages. Even well-versed Internet users whisper about the dangers of the ever-elusive "algorithm," but the question remains; what actually is an algorithm, and is it really the direct cause of such hate-fueled violence in the past two decades? The answer is more complicated than you may think.

To give a short answer, kind of. See, algorithms are tools created by programmers to personalize a user's feed. Whether it be a search engine, like Google, or an intensely individualized recommended page, like Facebook, an algorithm is designed to get you to click on links, and then keep clicking. It's not some evil entity bent on polarizing the youth with the power of the TikTok "for you" page, because, at the end of the day, it's just math.

That being said, there are also no regulations on what is too far for an algorithm to push to its users, which is where the problem comes in. Algorithms are formulas, that has been established. They don't have a moral code, or an ability to determine what may be hateful or politically extreme. As stated in their code, their one goal is to personalize and produce revenue. Without set limits, algorithms become hyper-personalized, which can lead to polarization.

Take my, (albeit minimal,) experiment with the YouTube algorithm. I created a guest Google account and entered the YouTube homepage. After about ten minutes of interacting with the algorithm, intentionally looking for key political concepts, I found myself going down a concerning rabbit hole of extreme right-wing rhetoric. From video titles such as "Why the Bible is Real" all the way to "Snowflake Liberal Gets Owned by Alex Jones," it became increasingly clear that there was very little the consumer has to do for the algorithm to work its polarizing magic.

Now, this experiment wasn't scientific by any means necessary. Not only was I the only person participating, but I was actively searching for politically charged keywords in video titles. It was my intention to exploit this pipeline. But imagine, if you will, a 12 or 13-year-old boy; freshly reeling from hormones, who loves to play video games, and has unlimited access to the internet. This kid opens YouTube for the first time, and clicking around decides to watch a gameplay video of Call of Duty, seemingly pretty harmless, right? Well the YouTube algorithm, following the revenue formula, recognizes the military aspects of Call of Duty, and recommends similar videos. Soon enough, this kid's homepage is full of videos about guns, militarism, and borderline fascist ideology.

That scenario may seem like a slippery slope argument, and it is, but it's true. The United Nations Office of Counterterrorism conducted a study aptly named "Examining the Intersection Between Gaming and Extremism" in which participants detailed their experiences on gaming and gaming-adjacent platforms (i.e Game chats, Discord, Reddit, Youtube, etc.) specifically in reference to "toxic or problematic behavior." 85% of participants said they had experienced such behavior on various platforms. Many said that YouTube and Twitch, (a live-streaming platform for video games,) were among the websites that push this "toxic" rhetoric. 11.1% of participants said that Twitch was actually the worst site for problematic behavior, citing instances of misogyny, racism, xenophobia, homophobia, antisemitism, and extremism.

Twitch and YouTube work in a similar fashion. Both are video platforms geared towards young people, with a wide variety of content. 77% percent of internet users ages 15-24 regularly use YouTube, and 89% of American parents say that their children, ages 5-11, use YouTube as well. On Twitch, 41% of its users are 16-24 years old. With so many young people on their platforms, the amount of hateful content should be of concern. Children are easily influenced by the media they consume. Their brains are not yet fully developed, leaving them vulnerable to hateful and even violent ideas pushed on the platforms that they commonly use. Anyone with eyes can see how this is a problem. The more difficult question, however, is what is the solution?

Is it legislation? If so, how do we balance content restrictions with first amendment rights? How would we enforce laws in the realm of the Internet? In the instance that a bill passes, would it be realistic, if even possible, that it actually is effective?

What about the website companies? Is there something they can do to slow their algorithms pushing extremist content to their users? How would they do that? Should they even be the ones held responsible? And what about the parents of the vulnerable youth, isn't it their job to enforce restrictions on their child?

As you can see, the task of putting responsibility on any one group is a difficult one. There will always be an argument as to why it isn't their problem, or reasons not to blame them. In all honesty, I don't have a definitive answer for who should find the solution, or even what the solution might be. It's a complicated matter, too complicated for this essay. What I will say, though, is that the only way we can find a solution to the prevalence of extremist belief is to work together. We have to have a little legislation, we will have to spend time holding companies accountable for the content on their platforms, we have to encourage parents to pay attention to what their children are consuming, and we must support education to teach children how to be loving, responsible adults, free of hateful ideas or violent behavior. Working together is the only way we can slow down the spread of extremism.

THE LIBRARY
Isabel Schmidt, twelfth grade

Belle shifted through the shelves, her fingers tracing along the plastic spines. The back corner was hardly ever used, the spines and covers becoming dusty and yellowed. To Belle, however, this was her favorite corner of the library. The request for *Occult History: All Countries and Counties* was strange, no doubt. Belle, however strange it may be, found the book through the catalog and went to find it. Penny, one of the other librarians on duty, had laughed and wished Belle luck. Adding on a humorous "We'll miss you!" as Belle disappeared from view.

It wasn't uncommon for the library to be quiet, but this corner was *extremely* quiet. Belle felt a shiver run down her spine as she turned a corner, not finding the book she had come for in the aisle. Her footsteps padded down the carpet, the only muffled sound in the building.

When she had left the front desk, students were studying and children browsing the shelves that were just a little too tall for them. Penny had been working on some of her own school work, taking a break every once in a while to place books in their proper pile. Belle, done with her school work and bored with her phone, had practically jumped at the chance to do something. Even if that meant going into the back of the library.

Not paying attention, Belle's finger caught the edge of one book, pulling it slightly out of the shelf. A loud grating noise followed, like a secret passageway from a movie. Belle stopped where she stood, looking at the book whose top corner was sticking out but with the bottom still snugly on the shelf. Curiously, Belle wrapped her hand around the book, pulling it down even more. The grating was back, and when Belle stopped pulling the book, the grating stopped too.

"What in the world...?" Belle whispered to herself, looking around for the source of the noise. When nothing was obvious, Belle left the book in its position and took a few steps towards the wall next to her.

It was covered in a maroon, velvet curtain. Belle tilted her head, there were no windows on this side of the library. Careful not to completely agitate the mothballs and dust, Belle used her hand to grab the edge of the curtain. It was thicker and heavier than she expected, and didn't move back as easily as she had hoped.

Slowly, the curtain moved back to reveal a small doorway set back into the stone wall. The doorway was kind of shapeless, with enough space between the wall and the door for a layer of rocks. The actual door was wooden, with a rusting handle that could have been gold at one point. There was an image carved into the wood, just at Belle's eyes. It spiraled inwards, a perfect circle.

"Oh my gosh, what am I doing?" Belle asked herself, aloud, as she gripped the door handle and twisted. The door squeaked open, easier than Belle had secretly hoped. It led to a hallway, a torch on the wall next to the doorway. She, regrettably, pulled out a lighter from her pocket and reached for the torch. She put one foot inside the doorway to reach the wooden, club-like torch.

A breeze blew past her, racing into the tunnel and almost knocking Belle off balance. The torch, only a few inches from her hand, lit in a blaze. More torches, lining the hallway with a few feet between them, lit as well. Belle peered down the hallway, dry stone as far as she could see and a bend, leading who knew where.

"This is *not* a good idea, especially with the *wind* that just came from *nowhere*," Belle's shoulders fell, and stepped into the doorway with the other foot. The door didn't close behind her, as she took another step. Belle was thankful that part of the movies were wrong.

Her boots, three inches tall and up to her ankle, tapped softly against the concrete ground. The passageway had a draft, blowing against her bare legs and over her chest. Her boots, once pristine white, were scuffed enough that Belle didn't mind when her foot caught on something and she knew there was a new scuff on her toes. Looking down, Belle held back her shriek.

A bone was laying on the ground, long and straight. A couple smaller bones laid around it, looking like a small shrine. Belle's eyes widened, her breath becoming fast and harsh.

"Oh my gosh, oh my gosh," Belle muttered over and over again. Her body was frozen in place, half of her saying to turn back and get Penny; and the other half saying to keep going, find out what is down there. The second half of her won, and she took a step around the bones to continue down the path.

"I would die in a horror movie," Belle muttered, the words echoing down the hallway. Belle stopped again after a few steps, she hadn't even spoken that loud. Taking a deep breath, full of crisp air, Belle took another step. The bend didn't reveal much, just another door. It looked almost identical to the first one, but the carving was of a flower. Five little petals on a singular line resembling a stem, almost reminding her of a magnolia.

The door handle was a flat, circular one this time, the same carving of a flower on the front. It looked gold as well, far less rusted than the door handle to the library. Unlike the door to the library, however, this door was much harder to open. The hinges didn't squeak, and the door wouldn't budge.

Belle leaned her whole body against the door, her hand still holding tightly to the doorknob. It shifted a little, just enough for Belle to know that it wasn't completely closed forever. She lifted her hip off the door, then used momentum to hit the door with her hip. It squeaked. So, Belle tried again. And again.

Everytime she bumped the door, it opened just a little bit further. Finally the door was open enough for her to see the edge of the room. It was circular, stone bricks with a high ceiling. Again and again, Belle pushed the door open. A desk was revealed, covered with decaying paper and old books. Again and again, until the door was open enough for Belle to slip through.

The room was larger than she had expected, the combined space of at least three study rooms. Only one other desk sat against the wall, the rest of the space open. Three bookshelves rested against the wall, each one filled with as many books as could fit. Some sat vertical, others stacked on top of each other. The covers were solid colors, looking like leather and paper.

A rug, shaggy and gray, sat in front of the shelves, the edges looked almost decayed. Belle could see, from her position by the door, that spots of it were missing as it sat under the leg of a chair. The chair was the same maroon velvet as the curtain in the library, the one covering the secret doorway. It was ornately carved, a dark wood to match the dark aesthetic of the room.

A window, large and open, filled the farthest wall. It curved with the stone, reaching about eight to ten feet along the bottom. The same maroon velvet fabric was draped halfway across the window, cutting the light in half. It was a strange diagonal, though. Like someone had tried to put on curtains, and after a lot of trying, had just given up. The sun shone into the room, allowing Belle to see all the dust swirling around the room.

Next to the desk across the room, very ornate and light wood, stood a door. The third door that Belle had seen on her adventure, with a different carving. This was very obviously a tree, a thick trunk and full leaves. The door looked in far better shape than the previous two, the floor in front of it cleared of dust.

Belle furrowed her eyebrows, eyes narrowing in on the quarter of a circle before the door. It was clean, the concrete floor without dust. Belle walked farther into the room, noticing a dresser out of the corner of her eye. The dresser was carved similarly to the chair and desks, and pushed against the door Belle had just walked through.

"Huh," Belle said quietly, studying the tree door ahead of her. "Someone didn't want anyone getting in through here."

The knob of the tree door turned slowly, causing Belle to panic. It was very obvious that someone had blocked the magnolia (or what Belle thought was a magnolia) door from opening, and the moved dresser and open door was a pretty good indicator that something was in there.

Making a split second decision, Belle ran across the room and slipped between the stone wall and the velvet curtain. There was a little alcove hidden behind the curtain, just large enough for her to fit in and move slightly.

The tree door didn't squeak, meaning Belle had no idea if someone was in the room or not. Above her head, a torch holder and torch sat, unlit. Belle reached up with one hand, careful to make as little noise as possible. Taking a deep breath, she wielded the torch over her head like a club.

"The door has been opened," one voice whispered, sounding like it was in the open space. "Who dared to open the door?!"

"We know the danger," another voice, higher pitched, whispered back. "None of us would risk it."

"Theresa, where was Carter?" the first voice whispered again, Belle could barely hear them. "I swear, if that little maggot-"

"It wasn't him! I'm sure of it," the higher pitched voice, Theresa, whispered back. She sounded almost frightened. "I was with him until early this afternoon. And I just left him to come and see you. There's no way he could have gotten all the way over here in such a short amount of time."

There was silence.

"And the door has opened from the other side," the first voice, who Belle was almost 100% sure was a man, hissed. "Someone has entered Ikapa. Someone who does not belong."

"Jason, we must tell the council!" Theresa was speaking at a normal volume now, surprisingly loud in the previously quiet room. "They'll know what to do!"

"The council will not be able to do anything, except for..." Jason trailed off.

Belle's breathing had evened out, her arms becoming tired from holding the torch for so long. She wasn't sure how long she had been standing in the alcove, but was sure Jason and Theresa were talking about something that the normal world had no idea about. She jumped when she heard a door slam shut, hopefully sealing Belle off from the two hostile people.

"Ikapa?" Belle mouthed to herself, testing the syllables on her tongue. It sounded familiar, like something said in passing. Racking her brain, Belle couldn't think of anything to connect the word to. She couldn't think of it in any book nor online in a magazine, she couldn't hear the word come from somebody's mouth or see handwriting displaying the word. Yet, it sounded so *familiar*.

A few more minutes went by, Belle lowering the torch to the ground but staying hidden, before she let go of the torch and peeked from behind the thick fabric. The air in the room was cooler, the light brighter than she remembered. The tree door was firmly shut, the magnolia door still as she had left it. The dresser still sat behind the door, looking so heavy that Belle was sure she couldn't even move it if she had tried.

Taking a deep breath and one last look at the tree door, Belle bolted across the room and through the magnolia door. The torches in the hallway were still lit, the fire casting erie shadows along the walls as Belle ran as fast as she could. The heeled boots were slowing her down, but she came around the bend and saw the open door to the library. Somehow speeding up, Belle pushed herself out of the doorway.

Spinning around the second she was out of the hallway, she pulled the door behind her. Belle pushed the curtain away, running back to the bookshelf to push the strange book firmly back into place. The grating sound was back, the stones (hopefully) replacing themselves to block the door. She wasn't going to check.

Belle, panting and sweating, sat down on the floor with her knees tucked up to her chest. Unsure of what she had just seen or heard, Belle sat there, replaying the moments in her head. And that's when she realized.

The torches were out when she closed the door behind her.

GRAY WAS MORE THAN A COLOR

Alicia Streeter, twelfth grade

The sun illuminating the gray
The gray of my room
The walls
Each appearing different shades
A kaleidoscope of gray
The sound of my computer
A gentle, guttural sound
Just like gray
My desk covered in
Dishes, old candy wrappers, wadded-up tissues and
Moldy apple cores
Gray is the mold growing into
The crevices, into everything.
My life, my lungs
I breathe gray.

The gray of the blanket
Warm and warn and musty
Like the gray hoodie on my floor
Dirty and damp and engulfing

That is my favorite hoodie.

Beauty in something as blah as gray
Beauty in you, Gray.

Scraping away the apple cores
Throwing away the hoodie
The tissues, the dishes
You, a friend

Everything was for the best.

DRAGONFLY
Chloe Taylor, eleventh grade

When I was eight years old, my grandma bought a brand new, bright and shiny, white, mini cooper. It was small, and it had one black stripe that went right down the middle. She filled it with plushies and action figures of colorful and sparkly dragons. Dragons in different poses and designs filled the dashboard to the point that if one more was added to the collection you wouldn't be able to see. Along with the dash, the back of the car was covered in stickers. Tinkerbell, Akittas, and cat stickers littered the back window, but my favorite was this pink lettering with a brighter pink dragon on top. It read, " Protected by Dragons," this sticker wasn't even the best part. The best part of this whole car was its name. My grandma named her bright white, mini cooper after my childhood stuffed animal Dragonfly.

This beat-up, off-white (though it used to be pure white), peppered in lint, ripped up wings, stitches in his underbelly, Beanie Baby, is Dragonfly. I've had him since I was two years old. Despite his name, Dragonfly isn't really a "dragonfly", he's actually just a dragon. Two-year-old me named him that because "he is a dragon and he can fly" and I thought I was a genius for coming up with this.

This little dragon, back when his wings still shimmered, and his color still popped, was a gift. Quite a long time ago, my family would meet up every Sunday for breakfast at that small mom-and-pop restaurant that I can't quite remember the name of. I don't quite remember getting Dragonfly either. I was two and was still probably in a high chair. My mom tells me that it was one of the waitresses that gave him to me. Apparently, poor Dragonfly was left behind by another little kid, and the waitress thought I was such a cute kid, that she decided to give him to me. This was the start of my love for dragons.

Similarly, my grandma was always very fond of these creatures (hence her car being filled to the brim with them). She would tell me stories about these fantastic beasts that once roamed the land. Her stories still stick with me today. She always had dragon memorabilia around her house. Plushies, figures, drawings, books—you name it, she had it. Her love for dragons was infectious, and I found myself captivated by her tales of their majestic presence and mystical abilities. I would spend hours exploring her collection, imagining myself soaring through the skies on the back of a dragon, just like in her stories. It was through her passion that I developed a deep appreciation for these mythical creatures and their place in our imaginations.

Wicca, (or people who practice witchcraft), is an alternative minority religion whose followers call themselves witches. Wicca and witchcraft are part of the larger contemporary which includes druids and heathens among others. This religion definitely differentiates itself from more mainstream religions, like Christianity, by celebrating goddesses as well as gods.

Also, Wicca lacks a formal structure, like a church, and instead focuses on more ritual and firsthand spiritual experience, rather than belief. People who practice this religion often participate in specific rituals, and practice some sort of witchcraft. While I cant say that my grandma was exactly a Wiccan, she did have similar beliefs, and practiced and believed in forms of magic.

My grandma could be best described as an "Animal Witch." I've never been able to find anything quite like this, but my grandma could talk to animals. It sounds totally insane, and when I tell people they don't believe me, my mom didn't believe my grandma either, well until she saw it directly firsthand.

This story happened before when I was still a baby, so I don't know exactly how long ago it was, but what I do know is that my grandma, my mom, my older sister, and my cousin were all tubing down the river. It was a beautiful day, the sun was shining and reflecting off the water's surface. My sister and my cousin were splashing each other, when my grandma looked up to see a bald eagle soaring above them. After my grandma saw the bird, she mentioned to my mom that she wanted a feather. That's when my mom looked up to see a single eagle feather float its way down from the sky, and right into my grandma's lap.

This wasn't the only "coincidence" of my grandma being able to talk to animals. Many years ago, when my grandma was still young, she was a bartender at a bar. One day, a police officer came into the bar while she was closing to tell her she should be careful walking home, due to some unsafe activities happening in the area. My grandma simply stated that she wasn't worried, saying she had a "bodyguard" to walk her home. When my grandma finished closing, the police officer watched as she stepped outside and a skunk scurried its way out of the bushes and began walking by her side.

When my mom was growing up she never believed anyone when they said that my grandma had this gift (well until the eagle story, that is). She grew up afraid of magic, of animals, and of these gifts, but my sister, however, was not. She was very passionate about animals and adored them. They loved and adored her back. My whole life I remember her being very good with animals.

My sister has told me that I'm like my mom in a way. She claims that I grew up scared like my mom. She told me that I'm very similar to my mom. I've never been scared of animals, but I wasn't raised around them like my mom and my sister were.

I know I'm not the only one with gifted people in my family. Pam Grossman, wrote a *New York Times* article about her gifted grandmother. Pam's grandma Trudy had "healing hands", and according to family lore, she once saved the life of a dying horse just by touching its flank. While Pam can't vouch for the variety of that story, (similar to me), she does know that she could cure a headache just from the touch of her hand.

My grandma calls what she does "Animal Speak." There's a particular book she uses to explain what she does, *Animal-Speak: The Spiritual & Magical Powers of Creatures Great & Small* by Ted Andrews. The book corresponds to a set of cards, similar to a deck of tarot cards, but not quite. The cards all represent a different animal totem, and each totem means something different. My grandma uses these materials to explain to others how she is able to do this, but It's still difficult to truly know how she does it.

My grandma loved every single animal, but there was one that she definitely favored over many others. Her favorite animals were dragons. You can imagine how ecstatic she was when she found out I developed an interest for the creatures. Ever since I got Dragonfly, dragons were my favorite. Once she found out about my new developing interest, every gift I received from her, nine times out of ten, was some sort of dragon memorabilia. Plushies, figures, drawings, books—you name it, She gave it to me. I still have all of the gifts she gave me, including my very own *Animal Speak* book.

My grandma was an incredibly gifted, and talented woman. She's influenced every single person around her, with her gifts, and her beliefs. Her books and stories still stick with me today. Through her passion, I developed a deep appreciation for these mythical creatures and their place in our imagination, and it all started with Dragonfly. From the Sunday morning, 14 years ago, to this very night when I lay down to sleep. Dragonfly has been there, and so has my grandma. The memory of her lives within him.

Jonas Carlson

2024 Literary Short Story

INSTRUCTOR INTRODUCTION: 2024 LITERARY SHORT STORY

Karin Killian

Our winter 2024 Short Fiction workshop was an advanced cohort of high school writers that met on Zoom on Saturday mornings from January through April. Because of this online format, students were able to participate from all over Northern Michigan. We also had a student zooming in from Virginia!

Our focus in workshop meetings was a combination of reading and discussing exemplary works of short fiction, discussions about the craft elements that make up stories, and how we can play with them to express different emotions and experiences, and writing time.

We also had fun playing with building stories together, out of characters we invented, and random pictures, and other writing prompts.

I loved noticing watching this group of teenagers develop a community of peers, even though we never met in real life. Art creates connection, and, with a little luck, these connections will go on to nurture the growth of more art!

The students in this group focused on writing new stories during the class time, but since they are all such pros, they also all have a wide variety of other writing projects they are working on. The following pieces represent only a small fraction of the immense talent in this cohort.

Keep Writing my friends. *I look forward to reading your books and seeing your movies!*

DARK/UNSEEN/SEA
Anabella Joya, tenth grade

(It's confusing to know how to feel at times like these. Sure, you rag and complain out at dinner with friends and you smile when they call, but don't want to talk to deaf ears. But, importance can't be determined by how often you talk, only by how you feel. Death isn't anything dark, really, not at first–a better metaphor would be the rug being pulled out from under your feet.)

It's imagined to be simple: five stages then you're done. But emotional stability fluctuates like ocean waves with no moon to guide them, and you are alone and adrift in the virulent sea.

The water is so cold and so dark you can't possibly imagine the craggy bottom, but the idea of jumping in is tempting just to see.

The moon is light and silver against the dark of your thoughts, salvation in physical form, but you don't know how to get up there; humans can't fly.

The fish swim around your floating form, worriedly nosing in at this obstruction on the sea surface, wondering if you're going to keep floating or sink down to the depths.

(You get the phone call in a car with your friends. Gasping, explaining in short words to stem their sudden worry, you get home to a house with a weird atmosphere and when the kitchen lights hit your skin after minutes in the dark, you feel too seen to be comfortable. Upstairs is a whole other maze. Where does your baby sister lie, does she need comfort yet? Does your mother know, does your father? How did your elder sister find out? There's a moment of stillness walking by your mother's room, you know she's going to feel things she hasn't before–and you know that you can't tell her.)

RIDE HOME
Written by Tess Tarchak-Hiss

Address
Phone Number

INT. CHUNKY AND CHEAP 2008 TOYOTA CAMRY - NIGHT

Four high school girls and one high school boy, all dressed head to toe in various cosplay, are jammed together. A GIRL DRESSED LIKE PAUL DANO, not from anything in particular, drives, as they all chat noisily, except for --

A GIRL DRESSED LIKE SNOOKIE, who moodily looks out the window.

> GIRL DRESSED UP AS ZELDA
> Shit, I really wish I asked for that Link's number. She was totally our age, right? God, I just love girls that look like boys.

> GIRL DRESSED UP AS PLANKTON
> You mean you like creeper 35-year old men with carpal tunnel who go to Comicon by themselves in full cosplay and can't grow a single hair on their bodies?

> CUT TO:

INT. YMCA GYM - FLASHBACK

The same five high schoolers sit in a circle on the gym floor, eating Chick Fil A, surrounded by all sorts of nerdy cosplays, furries and out-of-place Mennonites.

GIRL DRESSED UP LIKE ZELDA is staring and awkwardly smiling flirtatiously at a guy in a Link costume, who is very clearly a middle-aged man with a side part.

The other teenagers look at her with disgust.

                                                    CUT BACK TO:

INT. CAR - CONTINUOUS
                    GIRL DRESSED UP AS ZELDA
          Shut up, she was totally a masc
          lesbian!

                    GIRL DRESSED UP LIKE PLANKTON
          I can't believe they thought it was a good idea to
          have a Comicon at the Y.

                    GIRL DRESSED UP LIKE PAUL DANO
          Yeah, and was that a Mennonite wedding? I
          thought they only lived in that one state.

GIRL DRESSED UP AS SNOOKIE fiddles the car lock open and closed. GIRL DRESSED UP LIKE PAUL DANO glares at her in the rearview mirror. They make eye contact and SNOOKIE stops, and refocuses out the window on the snowy repetitive rural road whizzing by.

          BOY UP LIKE JOHNNY JOESTAR

          Okay so consider the 30 people at
          Comicon to begin with --

BOY DRESSED UP LIKE JOHNNY JOESTAR wiggles around in his seat, elbowing GIRL DRESSED UP LIKE SNOOKIE in her boob, completely oblivious. She glares at him, yanks off her bump it wig, revealing her bald cap underneath.

> BOY DRESSED UP LIKE JOHNNY JOESTAR
> (CONT'D)
> Thirteen out of 30 were furries.
> Since Comicon and the Mennonite
> party were in the same space, does
> that mean furries crashed the
> wedding?

> GIRL DRESSED UP LIKE PLANKTON
> Maybe they were Mennonite furries.

CUT TO:

INT. YMCA GYM AGAIN - FLASHBACK

The YMCA gym is filled with furries and Mennonites -- furries on one side doing stairclimbers and doing weird dance moves to rave music, on the other side a young Mennonite couple holding hands, surrounded by a huddle of wedding guests, all taking in the scene, perplexed.

CUT BACK TO:

INT. CAR - CONTINUOUS

> GIRL DRESSED UP LIKE ZELDA
> I felt bad though, when that lady
> ran out of the room crying. I mean,
> I would too, if I saw Twilight
> Sparkle hitting the griddy.

INT. THE YMCA GYM - FLASHBACK
A Twilight Sparkle Brony intrudes on the reception, griddying over to the bride's mother trying to get her to dance.

Frazzled and taken aback, the mother runs away from the function but accidentally lands up on the furry dance floor.

CUT BACK TO:

INT. CAR - CONTINUOUS

GIRL DRESSED UP AS PLANKTON, aux attached to her phone, turns on an atrocious HYPER-RAP MUSIC, which everyone sings the words to. GIRL DRESSED UP LIKE SNOOKIE groans.

> GIRL DRESSED UP LIKE SNOOKIE
> OH MY GOD. You guys play the same five freaking songs. And they all suck. Jesus, you have THE worst music taste. This sounds like clowns on psychedelics are sharting in my ear. If one more autotuned quirked-up Soundcloud white boy plays up in here, I'm jumping out.

GIRL DRESSED LIKE PAUL DANO shoots SNOOKIE a dirty look from the review mirror. GIRL DRESSED UP LIKE ZELDA rolls her eyes and exchanges a knowing look with GIRL DRESSED UP LIKE PLANKTON. BOY DRESSED UP LIKE JOHNNY JOESTAR, still oblivious to it all, just hums along to the song.

GIRL DRESSED UP LIKE PAUL DANO
What is your problem? You've just been a straight-up bitch. And I bought you Chic Fil A today too. God. That shit's *pricey* for fast food.

GIRL DRESSED UP LIKE SNOOKIE
I'm a vegetarian! I don't want Chic Fil A! You never ask me where I want to eat! Ever!

GIRL DRESSED UP LIKE ZELDA
Dude, you just like, downed a Spicy Chicken Deluxe, like, 20 minutes ago.

GIRL DRESSED UP LIKE SNOOKIE
It's my cheat day.

GIRL DRESSED UP LIKE PLANKTON
I don't think it works like that.

GIRL DRESSED UP LIKE ZELDA
And what are you even supposed to be?

Three months ago when we planned
this you were gonna be Randy Marsh,
but as a girl. And hot.

GIRL DRESSED UP LIKE SNOOKIE
I don't know, maybe cause those things are cringe? We aren't in middle school anymore, we aren't in the Pandemic anymore. People perceive us. Like, god forbid I don't know the freaking Sonic lore

anymore. I know we all became friends during the Pandemic, but going back to school has been...

An uncomfortable silence.

> GIRL DRESSED UP LIKE SNOOKIE
> CONT'D
> It's been weird. And different.

GIRL DRESSED UP LIKE SNOOKIE brings her knees to her chest. BOY DRESSED UP LIKE JOHNNY JOESTAR, finally sensing the tension, tries to be nonchalant and focuses on his phone. The THEME SONG TO ANGRY BIRDS blurts out. GIRL DRESSED UP LIKE PLANKTON yanks it from him.

> GIRL DRESSED UP LIKE PAUL DANO
> I know we're actually teenagers now, and in in-person school now, but that still doesn't give you a valid excuse to be mean. I know.

> GIRL DRESSED UP LIKE SNOOKIE GIRL
> DRESSED UP LIKE PLANKTON
> Do you even want to be friends with us anymore? Like honestly? We didn't even know why you were coming with us in the first place.

> GIRL DRESSED UP LIKE SNOOKIE
> I don't know.

The car is quiet while everyone realizes what SNOOKIE just said. A moment, then --

                    GIRL DRESSED UP LIKE ZELDA
          (to GIRL DRESSED LIKE PAUL DANO) Okay,
          well shit, let's drop her off first.

                    GIRL DRESSED LIKE PAUL DANO
          Yeah, your development is over
          right here anyway.

GIRL DRESSED LIKE SNOOKIE, upset, tries to not show it. She wipes
her eyes and one of her eyelashes unloosens, about to fall off.

                    GIRL DRESSED UP LIKE SNOOKIE
          Just drop me off here, I can walk.

                    GIRL DRESSED UP LIKE PAUL DANO
          I mean yeah, if you want to get
          out, sure.

GIRL DRESSED UP LIKE PAUL DANO pulls over fast. She unlocks
the doors. GIRL DRESSED LIKE SNOOKIE gets out.

EXT. RANDOM MIDWESTERN ROAD - CONTINUOUS

GIRL DRESSED UP LIKE SNOOKIE stands next to the four-foot
snowbank and watches the Camry pull back out onto the road, and skid
off into the distance.

Cold, she attempts to bundle up, but her Snookie clothing isn't doing it.
She puts her hand on her head and realizes something is missing.

                    GIRL DRESSED UP LIKE SNOOKIE
          (panicked, looking around)
          Shit, where did my wig go?

CUT TO:

INT. CAR - NIGHT
The teenagers in the car whip the Snookie wig around, belting a Sexyy Red song.

CUT BACK TO:

EXT. RANDOM MIDWESTERN ROAD - CONTINUOUS

GIRL DRESSED UP LIKE SNOOKIE huffs out a puff of air, and starts walking. She pulls off her fake eyelashes, and flings them into the night.

END.

8 MINUTES LATE
Kamea Helmstetter

This selection consists of the opening chapters of a novel in progress.

CHAPTER 1:

My therapist told me to start keeping a journal. That way, I could log my feelings and emotions and all that jazz, and see how they developed throughout the year. I think she meant for it to be sort of a loose, vent-y, maybe even angsty journal that chronicled my intense teenage emotions. I would have done that, really, because it sounds like a comical thing to look back on and reread as a 42 year old woman.

I would have done that, *really,* but I'm missing the loose, vent-y, angsty emotions. If that is a part of the adolescent experience, I guess I'm not an adolescent; I'm a middle-aged woman.

That's exactly why today is such a bothersome day. Lucky, the mangey, bug-eyed, loud little rat of a chihuahua my parents adopted two months ago, has had an affinity for purging the contents of his ginormous stomach in my room. He usually does it sometime in the evening, 8:00 pm at the latest, and I simply clean it up when I get home from taekwondo practice.

I'm not so lucky today, because he did it early, *early* in the morning.

My arm is growing tired from scrubbing the carpet, and the carpet is growing frayed from the repeated, soapy abuse I subject it to every night. I can almost hear it screaming, "Why? *Why?* Curse you, Erin! It's not even eight o'clock yet, I should still have time!" And then its cries being drowned out by that gross, squishy suds sound. *Eugh.*

I squeeze the nozzle on the disinfectant and it hisses in a way that would've been satisfying if it didn't send shivers down my spine. Why it does that I don't know, but I would've hoped to be immune to it by now. This procedure has been consistent for the past 6 ½ weeks, which I guess I should like, because of my taste for routines. Nonetheless, if it involves dog puke, I'm out.

But god, this is taking way too long. I wring out the magenta cloth I was using and let the soapy droplets fall to the carpet. I don't care if it grows mold later; maybe that'll deter Lucky.

I back up to the bedroom's door and gaze at my work. There were 3 puke spots in total, one of which was perfectly cleaned, and the other two were passable. It bothered me so intensely to leave it like this, but I've already spent 15 minutes on cleaning, and that is a sizable amount of time—big enough to cause a change to my daily routine, which is an absolute no-go. I dug my nails, bitten but with perfectly applied lavender polish, into my palms to cope with the horrid feeling of leaving my room in this state. I'll get to it when I come home for the night. *Eugh.*

I carefully pull out of the driveway, already feeling more at ease—the old, red, entirely unremarkable Sedan is the only place I can outlaw Lucky from. The inside smells of nothing in particular, but it's still weirdly comforting; the kind of scent you only notice when it's present. The faux leather seats are worn and have large, soft, human-shaped valleys from the repeated use of my friend and myself. The drivers' seat was marked in this way by me, because no one else is allowed to drive this car, and the shotgun seat had been claimed by my friend Ben. The back seats were hardly used. Should this sanctuary ever be disturbed by Lucky, I'll throw him back there unrestrained—as a science experiment, to see how he adapts, of course. Even though that's technically illegal in Michigan, I could find a loophole if I drove the 20 minutes down to the state border and into Ohio (I've put thought into this).

My old space heater clunks around in the seat beside me, only changing Ben's imprint on the seat slightly. He isn't very perceptive, so hopefully he won't notice.

My schedule had been shifted by the rat-dog by a margin of 15 minutes exactly. Usually that's how long it takes me to drive to school and get to first period, but if I wanted to lollygag at all, I would need to speed. My record is good enough to get me a job at UPS, which is how I measure driving success, but one day of speeding won't be too detrimental.

I accelerate the car and it protests, humming jerkily in the way it only did when I made it speed. The space heater's switch rubs against the back of the seat and turns off.

"Great," I grumble to myself, reaching over the inner console to turn it back on. I'm glad I dusted the console yesterday, because if I hadn't there would now be dust on my puffy jacket, and that would not be good.

The space heater makes a sound that reminds me of trying to awaken a teenager from a nap. The teenager isn't me, of course, because I don't take naps–they can easily destroy schedules if you oversleep–but everyone else I know makes that kind of sound.

I roll to a stop at a red light and pull out my phone to start playing music. The car lost its ability to pair with my phone a long time ago, so now I turn up the phone's volume as much as I can and set it on top of the space heater. "I'm Good" by The Mowgli's is playing. I don't know if I'd call this morning good, but whatever, Mowgli.

Speeding restored my schedule's balance by 7 minutes, but I would need to speed back if I wanted to fully fix Lucky's mistake. I walk off of campus and unlock the car, weighing the option in my head.

Twice in a day feels like tempting the fates. Granted, I don't believe in fate, but that's the kind of thing my mom would say, so I decide to drive home at the speed limit. My mom would also say that an 8 minute delay wouldn't kill me, and then my dad would chime in wryly, "It might kill someone, Jan. You never know." My dad's humor makes me anxious.

Driving at the speed limit–by which I mean 2 miles below it, as I like to–feels so much more peaceful and safe, even when the cars besides me are going 10 over.

"Say It, Just Say It" is playing now. I roll down the windows and holler out as many of the lyrics as I can remember. The frigid wind whips back in response, cold stinging my gums when I smile. I like singing, but I only really do it in the car–mostly because my voice gets raspy sometimes, but also because Lucky likes to howl along, and he just ruins it; I know he's just a dog, but that doesn't excuse his pitchiness.

I put the sedan in park and hop out, running up the driveway because that's faster than trying to pull up the windy pathway.

I jam my house key into its perfectly carved slot and open the door.

"Hey hon," my mom coos from the kitchen.

"Hey." I follow her voice, smiling at a new discovery–the sprint up the driveway, which at one point would've winded me, felt like nothing now. Must be all the taekwondo cardio. "Where's my uniform?"

"Right here, hon. Washed with only whites and folded the way you like it."

"Thanks," I reply. She probably thinks I'm thanking her for doing the laundry, but really, I'm thanking her for the attention to folding detail. These heavyweight uniforms are so temperamental when it comes to wrinkles!

As I go to reenter the kitchen, Mom shoves a warm, gooey chocolate chip cookie atop a napkin in my hands. "You didn't get much breakfast earlier."

"Yeah, because–,"

"Lucky. I know. Just your luck, right?"

"Good one," I grimace. I shift the cookie so that there's no chance of chocolate getting on my pristine taekwondo clothes.

She smiles her Julia Roberts-ish smile and rests her hand on my back, showing me to the door. "Lucky loves you, you know, just like a brother."

"Did your brother puke in your room?"

She purses her lips, as if deciding what answer to give. Finally, she shrugs. "Once. He had had one too many."

"I should bring that up at the next family reunion."

She chuckles, but cuts it off with an, "Absolutely not. Love you, don't forget to–,"

"Chamber and rechamber," I finish for her. Having a 2nd degree black belt for a mom comes with the perk of constant reminders about how to kick properly. It's endearing, if not a little violent.

"You got it, rockstar," she says. "Have fun."

CHAPTER 2:

I get to the studio–clunkily named ATA Martial Arts of Jefferson Springs–8 minutes late. I decide that changing in the sedan's trunk as usual would take too long (the only pro is privacy, but still, that's too many flailing limbs in so little space) so I take my uniform and the old, chocolate-stained napkin into the school.

As I walk through the entrance I'm shoved to the side. Amber Chen, Ben's girlfriend, scoffs.

"Out of the way," she growls, bearing her braces-covered teeth. The shade of green she chose always reminds me of spinach.

I don't pause to think about the interaction. I don't even pause to pick up the fallen napkin–not enough time. I head to the changing room and begin undressing.

I let my hands slip into autopilot and think over the interaction as I dress.

I'm used to a little sass from Amber, but only ever in snobby-girlfriend quantities. Not like what just happened, which was more like snobby-wife levels. She's always been a little wary of me, but I understand–her boyfriend of 2 years has a close female companion that is of equal, or maybe greater, attractiveness. I say "Maybe" because that's very subjective, and also because for a very long time, I thought Ben was gay.

I tie my belt around my waist, tight so that it will remain perfect, and I won't have to adjust it for a while. I tend to tie it a little higher up than most, so it makes it feel as if the bottom of my ribcage is being squeezed, which is a weirdly nice feeling. Kind of like one of those too-tight hugs from a family member who really, really loves you. I stop when it starts feeling like there's internal bone collapse, which family members never seem to know.

I got my Black Recommended belt–the one right before black, with the black, then yellow, then red stripes–a few months ago, and I plan on testing for my 1st degree black belt soon. Well, I guess it isn't as much of a plan as it is an intention; I'll need to actually study if I want to make it happen by the next testing date.

I stride out the doors of the changing room, absentmindedly tucking my shoulder-length hair into a ponytail that shoots out at the base of my neck.

I head over to Ben, who is staring off across the zebra mats. I plop down next to him and rest one arm over the chair's back. "How are you?" I ask.

No response. Ben continues his glare at his reflection, 30 feet away (I've measured).

I tap his shoulder, and he startles. "Did you not know I was here?"

His blue-green eyes, now focused on mine, are sort of misty. Not in a wet way, but in a distant way. "Uh... yeah, no, sorry."

I'm not sure how the answer could be both yes and no, but I know I wouldn't get an answer if I asked, so I move on to my next question. "Are you okay?"

He nods and rubs his eyes. "I–yeah, yeah. No, sorry, I'm fine. How's black belt stuff going?"

Ben is already a 1st degree, which I'm endlessly salty about. Luckily, by the time he tests for 2nd, I should be eligible too.

"It's good," I lie, lifting my arms to crack my knuckles.

"You think you're gonna test in April?"

I shrug my shoulders. "That's the plan. Are you going to help me prepare?"

He shrugs back. "You won't need it."

His gesture moved two stray, brown lox breaking off from his wavy hair pattern. I reach up to brush them out of his eyes, which clear as I do so.

He doesn't thank me, but he rarely does. "Is everything all good with Amber?"

Ben's eyes flutter wide for just a moment. "Yeah, of course. Why, did she say something?"

I think about it for a moment, then turn to watch the class happening on the mat. They're sparring, if you can even call it that–it's more like screeching as they do the sloppiest kicks ever, but at least they're trying.

"She just seemed mad about something. But if nothing happened, it's probably just random, and has nothing to do with you."

"I think she's on her period."

"Could be."

This is how most conversations between us flow; I say something long-winded and sometimes intellectually demanding, and he responds in a short, occasionally misogynistic way. I respond in a shorter, not misogynistic way, and we sit in silence until I repeat the cycle. I like the cycle a lot, because it's like a routine, and it's warm and fuzzy and comforting and not unfamiliar.

But... that silence is usually good. This time, it's boggy.

Ben pulls out a piece of paper and a ballpoint pen–he's always carrying one of those–and begins scribbling something out. I can't tell what, and I can't move to read it without it being incredibly obvious, so I rise to stretch my legs on one of the punching bags nearby, lifting my foot on top and squating with the other. This is another part of my routine here, stretches that make everyone else cringe at my hip mobility.

"You should stretch," I suggest, stifling a groan when my ankle pops under my weight. "Class starts in a few minutes."

Ben gazes up at me, before looking back to his paper. "I'm good."

I cluck my tongue and lower my leg, repeating the move on the other side. This one is the side that's always sore. "Okay."

He glanced back up. "Goddamn, pivot your foot. You're gonna break your knee." His writing becomes hastened.

I turn so he can't see me smile unless he looks at me in the mirror–he won't because he's so preoccupied with his writing. "Thanks," I say.

"More," he directs.

I twist back to face him and roll my eyes, shifting my foot again. "Better?"

"Yeah. Now you won't break it, just sprain it."

I push off the bag and onto the floor, rolling over my own head and onto my knees. "I love to see the confidence in others that simply radiates from you. It's very refreshing."

"Uh huh." He yawns and turns back to his reflection. Those same pieces of hair untangle and fall back in his eyes, but he doesn't move to fix them.

He *is* being weirdly sluggish, but with Ben, that can easily be chalked up to a night of poor sleep, or his own dog throwing up at 7:00. Although he doesn't value structured schedules as much as I do, you have to admit, that kind of thing can throw a wrench in just about anyone's gears.

A few minutes later, our instructor Mrs. Stry announces the beginning of our class. I start for the side of the mat, and when I'm not followed, I turn. "You coming?"

Ben rises to his barefoot feet, but just sways there. "I'm gonna take off."

"Take tonight off? Why?"

"No, take off. Like, leave."

My brow furrows. "Are you sure you're ok?" I settle into the line-up, my eyes still fixed on him.

He doesn't nod or shake his head, or really do anything that shows acknowledgement. He just tucks that piece of paper into his uniform's pocket and takes a step forward. "You're gonna be fine, Er."

I hate that nickname. He knows that.

"Well I know *I* will be." I cross my arms over my chest and sneakily adjust my uniform, which had been jostled from the stretching. "I'm asking about you, though."

Ben gives me that familiar grimace-y smile he does so well. "Don't worry about me."

"So are you going home?"

"Don't. Worry. About. Me."

"Ben."

"Er."

He pushes past Mr. Edison, the muscular red belt to my left, and onto the mat. As he moves, he grazes my shoulder with his hand.

"Don't call me that," I snap. I move to extend a hand, but he's out of my reach. He isn't telling me not to touch him, he's testing if I'll get out of line. "Just do whatever you need to do after class. C'mon."

I look down. He even put on shoes before this. What the fuck?

Mrs. Stry has a similar reaction. "Mr. Foster, what do you think you're doing?"

He plucks the letter out from his pocket and passes it to her. He leans at the waist so he can whisper something in her ear.

"Well, this is random," she mutters.

Ben shrugs away and this time, Mr. Edison knows to move.

"Ben?" I ask.

"If I wait, I'll talk myself out of it, and no one wants that, Er. Just let me be."

"Talk yourself out of what?"

He chuckles, and looks down at his sneakers.. When he looks back up, now through his long eyelashes, he exhales in a puff. "Out of what needs to happen for everyone's good. I've given it some thought, Er."

"Are you going to talk to Amber?"

"Er. I'll see you." He starts walking.

I can't break off of the class line up. I'm stuck watching, and he knows it. "When?" I call after him.

With his back still turned, he raised his hands over his head and made a heart shape with them. "See you."

"Ben!"

No response.

CHAPTER 3:

I didn't hear from him that night or the next, but honestly, I don't want to. I'm not thrilled with how he treated me last night–just blatantly ignoring me? Walking on the mat with shoes? No wonder Amber was so mad–it'd be easy with a boyfriend like him.

Ben has been known to go on long walks with little to no explanation, so part of me really did expect to see him come back after class ended, but that didn't happen. No one else even seemed to realize that he had been there at all that day, except for Mrs. Stry.

"Did Ben leave?" She had asked.

I nodded. "I think he got in a fight with Amber, ma'am. Probably went to smooth it over with her."

"Ah. Yeah, I bet."

On my way to school today, on time, I decide to call him. Dialing his number is muscle memory, and a relief, and it makes me feel like I'm not as bad of a friend as I thought.

"Hey. You've reached my voicemail. Thanks for calling me instead of just hunting me down at school, I appreciate it. I'll call you back sometime soon, maybe. Actually, probably not. Alright, it's been fun. See 'ya."

Beep.

Nevermind that, I guess. I feel a little defeated, but one thing is for sure... I will *not* be reduced to sending a pathetic voicemail with The Mowgli's playing in the background.

I turn up "Say it, Just Say It" and let it blast.

At lunch, I call again. Same thing.

I have taekwondo again tonight–I hadn't expected to see him, because he usually skips class on Wednesdays, but I know a little part of me still wanted him to come, if only so that I could beat him up for the other night.

I hop in bed and settle in for my nightly 15 minutes of scrolling on TikTok. 14 minutes later, I call again. Nothing.

I sigh. Okay, I'll voicemail. Knowing Ben, that could be the very thing he's waiting for.

"Uh, hey," I say. Ugh, why hadn't I thought of what I was going to say? "You've been kinda weird so I hope you're all good. Cool, bye."

I wait. No response.

I haven't seen Ben's mom in 5 months, and it's been such a nice absence. Emilia Foster, a 42 year old woman who I don't envy the lifestyle of whatsoever, is more like Amber Chen than her own son-insufferable and spinach-teethed. Seeing her at taekwondo tonight, watching from the viewing area while I practice my form, is like a gargoyle watching from atop a castle wall.

Mrs. Stry announces a water break, and as I head over to the water fountain, Emilia calls out to me. I hate confrontation so I convince myself that I don't need hydration and head over to Emilia.

"Hi Mrs. Foster," I greet. "How are you?"

"You know damn well how I'm doing," she spits.

I jump back, and bow over the edge of the mat. She knows she can't come across while wearing shoes, so I feel a little more safe here. "Sorry?"

"I feel like how any mother who just lost their only son would feel. Would you like to put that into words?" She spoke rapidly and bitterly.

Lost her only son? What?

I blink once, then twice. All I can do is repeat myself.

Mrs. Foster sucks in a deep breath through her brick-red lips, and then begins spewing words I can barely process. "I'm–my apologies, Erin. My appearance here is probably a little startling, right? Yeah. My bad."

I gape. What game is she playing? *Lost her only son?* After a few too many seconds I replied, "No, no, nothing like that. Sorry. Uh, can I help you, though?"

She stands, wobbling a little on her heels, and hands me a crumpled, tawny envelope. "I figure invitations like this are best delivered in person. All black, please. Oh, and could you bring a plate of those cookies your mom makes? They're lovely."

I can't force a response out from behind my teeth, so I just look down at the envelope. Would opening it in front of her be the wrong response?

"Alright, let's line back up!" Mrs. Stry calls.

Thank God.

I tear my eyes away from the paper and back to Emilia. "I'm sorry, I have to..."

"It's alright, just open it when you get the chance, 'kay?" She gives a respectful little head nod, which is so out of character it feels like a joke, and leaves. Her heels somehow clack on the carpet.

I tuck the envelope into my uniform, but I can't wait to open it, so I quietly dismiss myself from the mat and head into the employee's only area of the school–I'd been given access to it over two months ago, but this is the first time I've dared to enter it.

I open the door and quietly close it behind, sinking down against it. I tear open the envelope and scan the writing I recognize as Mrs. Foster's, from that time she wrote me a Christmas card. It was very passive aggressive.

In memory of Ben Foster, please join us in a celebration 4 him on March 23rd at Loving Arms Church, 228 Mahogany Lane, Jefferson Springs, Michigan, 48063. Service starts at 3.

Please bring a dish and RSVP ASAP. Thank you.

–The Foster Fam

QUILT

Laura Busick

I came to life
after hours of needles
and thread
and things called 'fat quarters'
I laugh through the patterns
woven in me
printed on me
stitched into me
and hold me together.

But my beauty isn't deceiving
I am a loyal companion.
I've been on top of wet grass
under the sun
the host of a picnic,

I've been wrapped around chilly fingers
by the fire,
I've been laid out on the carpet
for the baby
feeling her try to push herself up
with chubby fists,
I've been thrown in the backseat
"Just in case"
but I've also been shown
and admired

and loved.

So I've enjoyed every moment
of it all.

Jonas Carlson

2024 NWS Scholarship Winners and Highly Commended Works

In partnership with the Grand Traverse Regional Community Foundation

INTRODUCTION FROM GINA THORNBURY
Grand Traverse Regional Community Foundation

The National Writers Series Scholarship competition is made possible through a partnership with the Grand Traverse Regional Community Foundation and the generosity of several local donor partners. The partnership began in 2010 and the contest is held annually for high school students in our five-county region. Students are invited to submit in one of the four contest categories; poetry, fiction, non-fiction and journalism. To ensure an equitable process, a team of judges specializing in each of the genres completes a blind review, and selects a winner and runner-up in each category. Four $1,500 scholarships are awarded to the winners in each genre annually and $500 for the highly commended pieces in each genre.

Fiction

THE SECRET STORE ON FERN STREET
Emma Newman-Bale, twelfth grade

Highly Commended NWS William Montgomery Fiction Scholarship

Looking out the window of my apartment a shadow lurks over the city. Rain pitter-patters on the glass, not leaving a moment of silence. My tabby cat hides under the couch, meowing after every roaring thunder. However, I am not afraid of the storm like my cat. I embrace it.

Growing up I would run through the streets, forcing my mom to sprint after me. I wouldn't stop. Closing my umbrella I would open my arms to the rain that fell before me. Everyone always assumes that the sun is the happy weather, but not for me. The storms that have rolled in through the sky have released more dopamine in my little body than anyone could have thought. To this day, I am still entranced by the water that drops from the sky.

It has been years since I last ran through the water released upon the earth by Mother Nature. Not even thinking, my hands reach for the lilac colored raincoat. I look at the umbrella my mother bought me so many years ago, but it's left behind as I close the door. There is no plan of where to go, but I don't need one. My feet take me where they feel is right. Walking out the giant glass doors of the apartment complex, instantly a sense of relief comes over me. The rain melts my wavy hair and drips down my back. That doesn't matter.

A couple of strangers crane their necks, giving questioning looks. The lights of the city reflect on the puddles, forming their own unique rainbow. My feet start to pick up speed. I go from a jog, to a cantor, and then to a gallop. I make various turns and go down different blocks.

Somehow at some point, I went down an unfamiliar street. I look behind me and I no longer see the reflection of streetlights on the ground.

Coming to a halt, my eyes glance to the horizon. All I see is a tall brick wall, enclosing me on this strange road. Behind me, the street sign begins to glow and reveal itself.

"Fern Street," I mumble under my breath. Never have I heard of this street before. The rain starts pummeling down with all its strength. All of a sudden Zeus strikes the ground, causing me to fall back. Sitting on the cold wet cement of the sidewalk, I observe my surroundings. In the distance a street light flickers. The value of the sky gets darker by the second.

Quickly, I try getting up and dash to the only light in the darkening world. I keep stumbling over my feet, nearly tripping with each step. It took a minute to get to the dim streetlight, but looking at what it is illuminating makes my heart skip a beat.

A petite store with a blue and red open sign clearing me for entry. With nowhere else to go, I spring open the door. An older lady, no more than five feet, is behind the counter reading a mystery novel. She takes her reading glasses off and lets them hang by the beaded chain resting on her nape. We make eye contact and she has the prettiest eyes I have ever seen. Hazel, matching the color of sand, with a blue center that replicates the ocean surface. This woman is no ordinary person.

"It's about time you showed up," the old lady said, breaking the silence. My eyes darted around trying to figure out what place I just wandered into. No inch of wall could be seen as shelves reached from the ground to the ceiling. The shelving held hundreds of trinkets, leaving no room for anything new. It seemed that it was a weird type of vintage store. There are wooden figures, polished jewelry, old dolls, and some random objects that don't seem like anything but trash. Zoning out in a state of confusion, the old lady coughed. My head snapped back, facing her once again.

She grabs the side of her desk and slowly slides over to where I am standing. The table directly beside me is filled with art supplies. It would cost me a kidney to buy some of the items on this table.

"Take the paintbrush," she remarked and pointed towards a basket filled with them. What did she mean by "*the* paintbrush?" I was too scared of what was happening to disobey her beating eyes. My hand reached into the basket and it moved around trying to find the right one. Out of nowhere, I felt a spark when grazing the tip of my finger along the handle of a brush. My fingers closed around it and ripped the brush out revealing its shiny texture and an engraving on the side. Looking closer, initials were burned into the side of the paintbrush.

"E.H.," I whispered.

A tear rolled down my cheek, combining with the rainwater dripping down from my hair. I knew whose paintbrush this was and it broke my heart. It was my mom's, Eden Haueter, before she passed. My family knew how precious her "lucky" paintbrush was, but we were never able to find it. This moment felt like a fever dream.

"The brush was left on the doorstep of my shop one day," she calmingly stated, resting her hand on my shoulder.

"She used this on her deathbed, how on earth could it have ended up here?"

"All my stuff here is just left on my doorstep," she insisted, "I believe that everything has a purpose, it just needs to be discovered." Bringing the brush to my chest, a pounding headache erupts out of nowhere. Tripping over my feet I pass out on the floor.

My eyes flutter open revealing a bright light. Looking to my left I realize that it is the sun beaming through my bedroom window. Jumping straight out of bed and seeing that the paintbrush is on my nightstand, I begin to question reality. I'm still wearing the same clothes as last night and my hair is damp.

This couldn't have been a dream, thinking to myself. All day I stay in bed and just stare at the brush that lays before me. Thoughts rush through my head, unable to stay in one place at once. Reflecting on my Mom's last moments led me into a black hole and I was left engulfed by my own mind.

It wasn't until the next morning, not sleeping at all, that I was finally reeled back into reality. A knock on my door echoed through the silence of my apartment. My cat runs up to the doors and rubs his chubby body against it. I wish I could be a cat. Life seems so much simpler.

Peering through the little peephole, I see my landlord tapping his feet on the cement ground. I unlock my door just to be handed a yellow envelope labeled "eviction notice." I fall to my knees and he turns around without saying a word. I was so caught up in the whole paintbrush thing that I forgot to pay rent yesterday. I was already on thin ice and now I'm screwed. A chill runs through my spine and I only have twenty-four hours to get out of my apartment. I don't know where I'm going to go, but I know what I want to do. I grab the paintbrush off my nightstand, pull out a canvas from the closet, and take out the paints from my bookshelf. I unfold the easel that has been left in the corner of my apartment for the past decade, just collecting dust. I always used to paint with my mom when I was nervous about something.

I don't think, my hand just drives the wet paint across the canvas. Within minutes an image begins to form. The sky is a beautiful array of colors, and a flower garden with a vine-covered cottage fills the space. It was where my Mom and I always dreamed of living. Escaping the real world and living in peace surrounded by nature. Just us two.

After a couple of hours, without taking any breaks, the painting is complete. As I turn around to pet my cat, a flash happens behind me. Glancing back, the painted image becomes a window. A physical window to be opened. Slowly stepping over to the painting a breeze whisks my hair behind me. Reaching my arms toward the painting, it goes beyond where the canvas was supposed to end. Curiously, I stuck my head into the painting. I look around to see the cottage I painted standing before me. The flowers dance in the wind. The smell that flooded into my face sent me into a trance. I knew this is where I am meant to be. I didn't have anyone and now I'm losing my home. Sticking my head back into the window, a ladder appears welcoming me into this new world.

I begin to pack my belongings. Unsure of what will happen as soon as my full body enters the dreamland, I end up carefully throwing my stuff through. I decided to leave some things behind that I won't need anymore. Once everything I wanted was in the realm of my new life, I decided to take one last look at my apartment. It was still very cluttered, but it still felt very empty. I put my cat into a back carrier, grabbed the paintbrush, and made my way down the ladder. My feet met the ground and it sent a tingle through my whole body. It was where I was destined to be.

The paintbrush was a miracle. Never will I understand how I came to find it. All I know is my mom was an angel guiding me to my fate. I unpack my things and make the little cottage into *my* little cottage. As much as I wish my mom to be here and experience this place together, I was glad to see our dream become a reality. The sky darkened and I began to hear the pitter-patter of rain. I started thinking about that night when I met that old lady. So many questions and no answers. I can live with that though. I wouldn't change where I am in the world. The rain starts to pound harder on the roof. I swipe the same lilac colored raincoat and open the door. My cat meows at me, but I give him a treat and he returns to his bed placed on the windowsill. I close the door behind me and start to run. I'm galloping through the flowers, taking a few rests to admire plants I've never seen before. The water splashes off my head, soaking my hair right up. The scent being emitted reminds me of all the moments I spent dashing through the rain with my mom.

I stop running and just look to the sky. My eyes struggle to stay open, but I remain gazing up. The sky is painted in various shades of blue and gray. I think of how I got here. The rain. It all started with the rain. It led the way to the place of my dreams. I hope in every universe I am able to reach this place.

I will always and forever stumble back into the little secret store on Fern Street to reach this paradise destination.

OVER THE EDGE

Kaitlyn Andrews, twelfth grade

NWS William Montgomery Fiction Scholarship First Place Winner

Lily hadn't meant to take it. Honestly, after her last stunt she had resolved to keep a clean reputation from then on, but the opportunity had been so tempting. Too tempting. The little gold key hung on its hook, swinging gently in the autumn breeze, clinking deliciously with each sway. It practically begged her to reach out and grab it. It had been too easy.

She had planned on returning it, she could come in the next day, say she'd found it on

the street and the shopkeeper's eyes would likely fill with little tears of gratitude, nestled into the wrinkles of his sweet sun worn face. He would thank her repeatedly and maybe even offer a reward for such an honest bystander. Honest. Hah.

Lily was many things but honest was not one of them. There was no denying that now. Despite the heavy load of shame that settled atop her shoulders, she turned the key in the lock and crept deftly into the pawn shop, her feet silent and her spirit sagging. Reviewing the goods with an expert's eye she instantly recognizing which items held more value than the others. She reached out with shaking hands for an antique music box nestled under a fabric spool, a priceless piece. She doubted even the owner knew of its worth. Just as her fingers began to brush the smooth porcelain base an arm shot out of the darkness clamping her wrist in a gentle yet iron

grip. "Now my dear," a cracking whisper of a voice murmured "I don't believe that belongs to you."

Lily let out an involuntary gasp as she jerked her head up to face her captor. Her eyes met that of the gentle shopkeeper. "We close at 8:00" he told her softly "but I think you knew that."

She stared dumbly unable to speak.

A raspy sigh escaped the old man's lips as he stared at Lily. She was shocked by the sadness conveyed in his wise brown eyes. "Please have a seat" he said gesturing to a nearby chair.

She sat down hesitantly perched on the edge of the seat, awaiting condemnation. Staring up into his mournful eyes she felt her own fill with tears. The moisture balanced on her lashes, threatening to spill over. "I'm sorry" she whispered.

"I know my dear" the shopkeeper replied, a note of tenderness in his voice as he handed her a handkerchief.

She sniffled and wiped her face gratefully on the cloth.

The shop keeper waited patiently while she composed herself.

"Thank you" she mumbled, reaching out to hand him the damp handkerchief only to hesitantly pull it back when he waved his hands in a negatory gesture.

"You keep it, I have plenty."

She was struck by his kindness "why...." she began, stuttering as her voice got caught in her throat, "why are you being so nice to me?"

"Why wouldn't I be?" He asked looking genuinely puzzled by her question.

"I broke into your shop." She whispered her voice barely audible "I was prepared to steal from you, and the only reason I didn't is because you caught me."

He nodded along with what she said, frowning a little at the end "now there's where I think you're wrong" he said gently. "I believe you have enough good in you that you would've made things right once you came to your senses."

Lily was taken aback "Then you don't know me. I'm a bad person, I've stolen plenty of things, plenty of times!"

He nodded again "yes I'm sure you have, but that doesn't make you a bad person."

"But I am!" She protested, surprised by her deep urge to convince this man of her guilt, "I've done so many terrible things and I've had so many chances to make them right but every time I've just ran away!" Tears threatened again "you wouldn't even be speaking to me if you knew some of the things I've done." Lily's shoulders slumped, and she tensed herself for the rejection that was sure to come.

"May I tell you a story?" The shopkeeper asked.

Lily stared up at him. Out of all the things she had anticipated him to say this was not one of them. She nodded numbly after a moment. What could it hurt?

The shopkeeper's eyes twinkled as he began his tale, face shifting into an expression that can only be described as melancholy as he was transported back to a time long past.

"When I was a boy I grew up in a little town called Cambridge" he told her. "My dad was often gone, so naturally I would get into a bit of trouble while he was away, as young boys do."

"My choice of company was a gang know as the Vipers." He chuckled, "Those boys were as wild and free as the wind itself and I enjoyed the rush that accompanied their escapades. I never questioned the nature of my involvement with them until one unforgettable evening in late July."

"It was the hottest day I can remember. The air itself seemed to be sweating as we walked along the riverbank. The water was ice cold with a current that raged constantly, destroying everything in its path. It terrified me, but per usual what terrified me enchanted the others. There was a peak overlooking the depths of the river where the rapids rushed at breakneck speeds, that was our base. Monty Mcwarnis, the leader of our group, decided that day that it would amuse him to see somebody jump the gulf."

"'I'll bet not a single one of you is man enough to jump the river' Monty taunted his eyes gleaming. A couple of the younger boys chuckled thinking him jesting, but the more experienced of our ranks knew that when Monty locked onto something it was nearly impossible to detach him from it.

'You think it's funny, do you?' he asked them, turning a withering glare on the newly initiated Robby. 'Why don't you go ahead and give it a try?'

All ounces of humor drained from Robby's little face as he shook his head vehemently, too startled to speak.

'Oh, come on!' Monty insisted gesturing to the cliff 'it's only a couple feet, I could jump it with my eyes closed.'

'Then why don't you?' I heard a voice say that I was shocked to recognize as my own."

The shopkeeper turned his gaze on Lily "I've thought back on that moment a lot" he told her. "For many years I believed I spoke up to help little Robby, but now I think I did it for me. I had been sick and tired of Monty running his mouth and never doing anything to back up his talk. I remember thinking that even if I went down, at least Monty would go down with me."

Lily nodded knowingly, the concept wasn't too foreign for her to grasp, she had run into similar situations herself. "So, what happened?" she asked. Even in her gloom she was enthralled by the tale and charmed by the enthusiasm of its speaker.

The shopkeeper smiled at her. "Well Monty was not all that happy to be challenged. His attention was on me in an instant, all thoughts of Robby forgotten."

"'Why don't I what?' he snarled.

'Jump over the gulf with your eyes closed.'

Monty's eyes flashed angrily 'who do you think you are?' He asked me 'am I not still the leader of this gang? Nobody tells me what to do!'

I had just looked at him and shrugged 'I'm not really telling you what to do.' I said, 'I'm just asking you to demonstrate what you said you could do in the first place.' 'Besides,' I reminded him 'it's only a couple feet.'"

"The boys began to murmur around me and many of them agreed with the notion of Monty jumping the river. A chant came out among them which soon grew to a deafening roar. There was no way Monty could back down without looking like a coward."

"'fine!' He announced waving his hands for silence. He was the picture of nonchalance, but I could see the fear in his eyes. And the anger. 'But' he added 'if I'm going, you're coming with me.'

'fine' I had said mimicking his casual tone, trying and failing to calm my racing heart 'how about you show me how it's done?'

Monty's face went ghostly pale, but he quickly covered it up with an obnoxious guffaw 'not a chance' he told me 'There's no way I'm letting you chicken out.'"

"I knew I was in deep then and there was no way of getting out. I searched my mind desperately for an excuse, a reason why he should go first or why I shouldn't go at all but everything I came up with make me sound weak, pathetic. So, at the price of my pride, I squared my shoulders and marched myself to the edge of the cliff. Once I reached the edge, I took one final look back at the boys knowing that no matter what Monty and I would jump or be forever humiliated. I took a couple steps back, preparing myself for a running start to jump over the ravine. My feet slammed against the ground as the cliff grew closer and closer until I was almost on top of it. I watched as my feet left the edge only to be suddenly jerked back by a powerful grip on the back of my shirt."

"'What do you think you're doing boy?' A furious middle-aged man demanded sticking his face close to mine 'do you have a death wish?'"

"I stared up at him for a moment looking into his red, slightly wrinkled, angry face and then I look at the river raging below and the devastating jump of 20 feet that I had just been prepared to take all for the sake of my pride and I knew without a doubt that this man had just saved my life. And with the shock and realization of how close I'd been to death came an overwhelming wave of emotions that ended with me falling, sobbing uncontrollably into the arms of my rescuer."

The shopkeeper blinked up at Lily, tears gathering in the corners of his eyes at the memory "I never went back to the gang after that" he said.

"The man who saved me was named Henry Clipper and he became more of a father to me then my own had ever been and remained that person until he died five years ago" ,his voice was choked with emotion, "I will never forget that day when he saved me, twice."

"Twice?" Lily inquired uncertainly.

"The first was when he lugged me back over that cliff, and the second was when he pulled me out of that lifestyle." "He saved me from the person I had become and the person I would've been if I had somehow survived that fall. And now when faced with someone that I see myself in I'm trying my best to do the same."

Lily looked down at the cold hard floor "you don't know me" she said at last.

"Ahh but I do" the shopkeeper replied tenderly "I know the look in your eyes and the longing in your spirit and the emptiness in your heart and I can tell you right now that what you're doing isn't going to fix it."

"Then what will" Lily asked her own tears resurfacing "nothing will ever help me escape this life. I can't escape the decisions I've made, the things I've done."

He pondered this for a minute "you can't change the things you've done" he agreed "but what you can change is the things you will do."

"I don't know how" Lily admitted. This was the only life she had ever known. "If I may offer a suggestion?" The shopkeeper asked gently.

Lily looked up at him, unsure of how he could possibly help her.

"I'm getting old" he told her "I can be forgetful at times, and I love this old shop so much I can't bear to see it go down with me. I can't afford to pay you much, but it would be steady and in a couple years, if you're willing to stick around, and wouldn't mind having me for company, you could take it over. I think you'll find running this little place fulfilling in many different ways."

Lily stared at him for a moment completely and utterly speechless "you want to.... hire me?"

"Yes, that's what I'm saying" he said warmly.

"But why.... why would you ever.... how could you?"

The shopkeeper smiled patiently "I think you'd be a nice addition to my little business" he said. Then in a conspiratorial tone he leaned in and whispered, "And between you and me I have been a little worried about thieves lately."

Despite herself a tiny chuckle escaped Lily's lips which soon became a laugh. The old man joined her and somewhere along the line her giggles turned into sniffles which soon became sobs. Strong comforting arms pulled her out of her hysteria, and she turned her bleary eyes onto that of the shopkeeper's "I don't even know your name" she confessed.

He smiled "it's Joshua, Joshua Colman."

"Thank you, Mr. Colman," she whispered, "whatever happens I do believe you've pulled me back over the edge."

Journalism
THE STRUGGLE FOR SOBRIETY

Eliana Hermel, eleventh grade

NWS Judith Lang Journalism Scholarship Highly Commended

Scott Scholten had his first drink while he was in elementary school. "It gave me an instant love and gratitude," he recalls. "It was like having a warm blanket wrapped around me." After his first sip, Scholten kept coming back to it. The sweetness of the bitter drink was like an old friend saying, 'Welcome home.'

To understand how he got to this point, let's rewind the tape a bit.

Long before he began working with addicts himself, Scholten was born into an alcoholic household. Both of his biological parents were drinkers, which led to his biological mother giving him away at 11 months old. "[My biological mother] let me go on to hopefully have a better life," Scholten mentions. "[However], what my mother growing up didn't realize is that... I had a great risk of becoming an alcoholic or addict because of my bloodline." Although his adoptive mother gave him quite a good life, her nonchalant attitude towards alcohol gave Scholten an unusual perception of it. She would regularly have a drink with meals, or even drinking parties with friends. By age 12, Scholten was able to mix up her friends' favorite drinks, such as martinis or Manhattans. "What my mother didn't know is that it wasn't age-appropriate," he reveals. Because of his early access to alcoholic beverages, Scholten had no problem trying a bit for himself. There was no fear or dislike; due to his genetics, the drink instantly stimulated him with feelings of comfort, calmness, and peace. The drink continued to do so for the next 31 years of Scholten's life.

Just a few short years after that first sip, Scholten realized that he had become addicted. "I knew early on as a teen that I had to hide my drinking," he admits. "That's part of the addiction; you lie about your amount of use." Although he hid his drinking, the addiction didn't prevent him from working. In fact, it actually influenced his work life. "It's a really expensive habit," Scholten addresses. "I had to work really, really hard to afford the amount of alcohol that I would drink." Scholten was what is considered a 'functioning alcoholic,' where he is still able to maintain a stable job and family life despite his addiction. While he was able to physically be there for his family, the addiction was always at the forefront of his mind. "Even though I made it to all the games, plays, and musicals, if you got close to me, you would've smelled alcohol," Scholten recounts. It stayed that way for a long time, until it went too far.

Eventually, Scholten found himself being charged with drinking and driving offenses. "One day, the judge goes, 'You're going to either die or go to prison because of your alcoholism,'" Scholten remembers. "'But, I can help you become sober if you want.'" Being willing to do whatever was necessary, Scholten accepted his judge's challenge to become sober.

After the judge introduced him to the Treatment Court for Alcohol and Drug Addiction, he was able to find a sponsor. A sponsor can assist a recovering alcoholic through their journey to sobriety. "I fell into the same model of being around like-minded people, [where] we wanted the same thing," Scholten explains. "One: we wanted to be sober. Two: we didn't want to go back to where we were, because we knew that it either led to death or jail." While he was motivated by a fear of the consequences, the guilt that came with recovery also took a toll on Scholten. His family happily supported him through his journey, but he still felt liable for the experiences he put them through. "There wasn't a day that went by that I never felt an immense amount of guilt and shame because I had to hide my use," he reveals. "I always felt like I was letting [my family] down by not being the perfect dad or the perfect husband." However, being in the Treatment Court also gave Scholten easy access to therapy. The counseling he received helped him through the process.

After struggling within the binds of alcoholism for 31 years, Scholten finally won. He became sober 14 years ago, and he didn't take his new-found freedom for granted. "I am now employed by the GTB [Grand Traverse Band of Ottawa and Chippewa Indians] in the behavioral health department as a peer recovery coach and mentor," Scholten beams. "That means that I'm able to give back to my community and help others to learn the pathway of recovery and sobriety." By using his past experiences, Scholten has been able to empathize on a very personal level with others who are struggling with similar addictions. "He gives a lot of his own personal time and energy into the community as a whole," Scholten's manager, Kathy Tahtinen, shares. "He participates in events, he takes phone calls all hours of the day and night, he walks alongside the people that he serves and works with them to try to get them where they need to be."

By serving recovering addicts, Scholten has been able to witness lives being built up again. "[They're suddenly] getting their jobs back, getting their children back, paying for homes, and [even] paying for cars," he praises. "I don't ever expect a thanks or a hug. Just seeing that family dynamic come back and children loving their mom or their dad again [is enough]."

His passion for helping others has translated into a passion for change: both for his clients and himself. "The more awareness we bring to this, the more we normalize the fact that it happens and recovery does work, the more we talk about it and the more we celebrate it in public, the greater effect it's gonna have," Scholten expresses.

THE DIGITAL DIVIDE

Kailyn Groves, eleventh grade

NWS Judith Lang Journalism Scholarship First Place Winner

Every year, Central holds a PSAT day for high school students. Traditionally, the test has been given on paper, but there have been many changes to the format in recent years. When COVID initially forced staff and students to stay home and quarantine, students were not able to take the test, and it was uncertain when and how makeup tests could be done. In response, College Board, the organization who designs these standardized tests, created a digital version of the test so students could remain at home, and it was successful. As a result, the College Board started to play with the idea of making all of their tests digital in the future.

After a few years of trying digital testing with freshmen classes, it proved to be a success. Because of this, College Board opted to expand digital testing to all grade levels this past fall. All 9th-11th graders at Central took the PSAT digitally for the first time, but it wasn't without its problems. Due to some technology issues, some students and staff struggled to access the test before nine in the morning. "You have to keep in mind that there were over 500 high schools in Michigan that were given that same test, at the same time, on the same day, and the College Board had not done that yet," Assistant Principal Brian Guiney states. "It's logical that there was some lag time, but I know that was stressful for us." Despite the technology issues in the beginning, the test flowed smoothly without many other issues.

October's testing brought both positive and negative perspectives and some strong opinions, especially in the pacing. "I think that it is a lot more stressful for students," Isabelle Cox '27 claims. "Last year, I had done it on paper, and I felt like that was a lot easier and better." Students tend to worry about how much time they have when taking standardized tests, and the digital PSAT uses a timer at the top of the program that counts down the time remaining in the current section. For some, the timer is anxiety-provoking, while for others, it's a helpful tool to use when they are finished with the test or just starting. "We are always on screens [anyways, and] the timer shown at the top [makes] us rush and not think clearly," Cox shares.

Some students did find the digital format better for their own needs. "It just felt faster," explains Elaina

Chippewa '25. "Instead of me staring at a piece of paper, I could easily go to the questions I wanted to...and come back to them when needed."

Teachers seem to have a more positive attitude toward digital testing based on the advantages digital assessments bring. "I think it's a good thing," Science teacher Mary Boulanger argues. "I also like that students can move along and then their test will automatically start the next [section] so that they don't have to sit and wait for everyone to start and end at the exact same time." Administrators and other staff members are also thankful for digital testing because it removes the time spent going through instructions and organizing thousands of testing materials. "The number one benefit for the digital tests is [that] we don't have to organize, pass out, collect, and then ship a bunch of paper materials back to the College Board to be graded," Guiney remarks. "It saves money on our end and it also is much less of an environmental footprint for Central and the College Board."

The digital PSAT will be established for upcoming years for all high schoolers registered to take the test.

According to the College Board, it's mandatory to take the test digitally from now on unless they decide otherwise. In the foreseeable future, students will most likely be sent back to class after the test and will continue until the end of the school day, regardless of whether a student has accommodations. In past years, students had the rest of the day off from school. "We have to meet a certain amount of instructional minutes over the course of the 180 day school year in order to receive funding from the state of Michigan," explains

Guiney. Even though this is a downer for students to have to go back to class, the day would not "count" towards the required attendance and we would have to make up the lost time later in the year.

To get data on what the general consensus is for this issue, the Black & Gold Quarterly polled Central students about their opinions. The overall results showed that more students favor digital testing rather than paper, but when it comes to the class breakdown, the freshmen class was the only group that overwhelmingly preferred digital testing. In comparison, upperclassmen seem more split, with seniors preferring paper testing significantly more.

Standardized testing and the new format for the PSAT has been a hot-button issue for many Central students this year. The way testing will be formatted now and for the years ahead is the future for all of us, and hopefully in time, it will be a better experience overall.

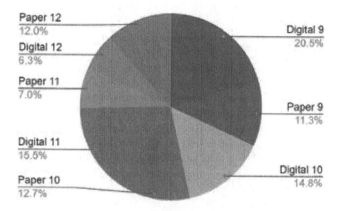

When taking a standardized test (PSAT, SAT, etc.), which method do you prefer

146 responses

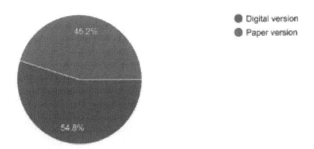

Description of Graphic: A recent Central testing survey indicates the majority of underclassmen prefer digital testing, while upperclassmen are more split.

Poetry
SIRENS AT MOONRISE

Kendra Courturier, twelfth grade

*NWS Robert and Marcy Branski Poetry Scholarship Highly
Commended*

a bird slices through the dome in the half-dark and, distant,
sirens at moonrise.

breaking news broken news broken glass

and, somehow,
violins and cellos and piano notes on high spilling out on the grass.

all I ever wanted was another butterfly year, a hope,
but instead, I'm reconciling futures with the fate of birds against glass,
dreaming in reverse.

APOLOGIES TO EACH ERASER

Lola Russell, eleventh grade

*NWS Robert and Marcy Branski Poetry Scholarship First Place
Winner*

I want to thank Each eraser,
On the end of each pencil, That I've worn through
In the first months of school Each year.

Thank you
For rubbing away each mistake That dented the paper I wrote on As I
　quickly
And half-heartedly
Dragged the pencil along the page.

Thank you
For being the factory-made solution I needed Each time the shiny
　graphite revealed
I had done something wrong.

But, Really,
Why did you have to do that? It was because,

I took your help for granted, Over and over again,
Even when you were scraped down to a millimeter And there was
　evidence,
In the form of deep pink wisps,

Around my feeble attempt at a response On the paper.

And as I continued To erase,
Any and all, Misspelled words
And incorrect punctuation, The moldable metal
That connected you
To the rest of the wood
Began to scratch against the paper.

I realized then
That all I could ever focus on Were my responses,
My handwriting filling the lined paper, My words being written
Exactly as we had learned in Kindergarten.

And I'm sorry that I Decided who you would be
Right when you left the flimsy cardboard box And replaced you
When you could no longer Be the quick-fix
For everything I had done.

Nonfiction
MY TRUTH OF TUNA CASSEROLE

Lucas McSwain, twelfth grade

NWS Leslie Lee Nonfiction Scholarship Highly Commended

"Bonehead!" my Grandpa would yell at me and my siblings when we were idiots. The best way to have described him was him being logical, funny, and generous. He was undoubtedly a smartass, so much so that no one debated him because they would lose. But one day a young 2nd grade me broke a small crack through that iron wall, and it was all over a conversation about bees. He talked about how male bees attacked with their stingers while I was in the living room. I tilted my head back and remarked "But male bees don't have stingers." My grandpa responded, "Yes they do." Right then and there, it became a dispute of "Uh-huhs" and "Nuh-Uhs" flying back and forth. I delivered the finishing blow... "Google it!" To everyone's surprise (not mine) I was right. Male bees do not have stingers.

Those are the fond memories. The smell of tuna casserole in the oven, and the humidity engulfing the house. The glass pan coming out of the oven and being set on the rusted stove top. I open the dark wooden cupboard door and grab out old glass plates. The pan is set on the dinner table as I set down the plates at each seat. The big spoon breaks the crisped top, then slops it on each plate. I put a bunch of salt on it until it's too much. I never really know how to proportion the salt so I have to stop sprinkling it on. Dinner is normally at 5:00, no, 4:00pm. You have to remember my grandparents were oddballs when it came to their meal times.

As much as I love tuna casserole, it's quite scary not knowing how much mercury my family and I have consumed from the tuna. A little fun fact is that mercury amounts found in tuna is volatile and could be increasing (Kirchner, "How Worried Should You Be about Mercury in Your Tuna?" *Consumer Reports).* Mercury levels can vary significantly between different types of tuna and among different brands. Each tuna can may vary in levels of mercury. Which, in case you didn't know, could have detrimental health effects on pregnant women and children especially. The FDA has guidelines that recommend limits on tuna consumption for pregnant women. There are typically two types of tuna commonly used in canned tuna, Albacore and Light tuna. Albacore tuna typically has higher mercury levels. Just some of the places that mercury impacts are: the nervous system, the immune system, and the digestive system (World Health Organization).

A leading cause for mercury found in tuna, as well as other species, is thought to be pollution from industrialization seeping into the oceans. It's said that reducing human activities like fossil fuel emissions can decrease the mercury contamination in the oceans. Different oceans and regions have different levels of mercury; contamination is higher in more industrialized areas. There have been recommendations on the amount of tuna, as well as other mercury containing fish should be consumed in moderation (Kirchner, "How Worried Should You Be about Mercury in Your Tuna?" *Consumer Reports*). From what I know, neither me or my family haven't been effected from mercury; even though I've been eating tuna all my life.

When I was young and after my parents split and I moved up to Michigan, one of the places my little sister and I would stay was at my grandparent's house. I would say that they were a big part in raising me. I am very grateful for them and how kind they were to us. They would always make sure we were fed and not cooped up inside. Granted, it was one of the few places I had to sleep on the floor, but I didn't mind it. My sister and I were such brats, we bickered and whined, and were very picky eaters. Then again, whose right is it to deem my sister and I "brats." We learned to expand our taste by going in the garden and stealing already grown food like onions and chives. Regardless, my grandparents still put up with us.

I wonder what the most important ingredient is in tuna casserole? Well, that special ingredient is going to become inaccessible. In 2010, 1.5% of the bluefin population decreased.

The decline doesn't seem noticeable, but it's a sign. Conservation experts and sushi chefs have different opinions on people eating bluefish tuna. Go figures, they both have opposite needs of tune. Some think it can be sustainably managed while others say it should be completely avoided (can you guess who?). Organizations like the Monterey Bay Aquarium's Seafood Watch, recommend avoiding all bluefin tuna species due to concerns about overfishing and by-catch issues (Jean Trinh "Should We Be Eating Bluefin Tuna?" *Los Angeles Times*). We have caught too much tuna, the most common fish found in sushi (so enjoy while you can). What really doesn't help is the high demand for tuna; it's one of the most common fish found in sushi and tuna companies. Who knows, maybe tuna casserole won't be the same in the future. It's not like bioengineering meat will become a thing.

The population deficit of bluefin tuna, and even the potential health implications from mercury exposure still hasn't changed my appetite for tuna casserole. Tuna is just another food that we don't really think about how it got to the dinner table. To be honest tuna alone kind of has a messed-up history and current status. Will that effect me eating tuna from now on?

Absolutely not. I'm going to take the stance "ignorance is bliss" on this one. I'd rather not contemplate all of this while I'm at the dinner table gobbling up tuna casserole.

I learned a bit from my grandparents: How to take care of a garden, utilizing a computer, cooking, how our government works, and so on. But what I wished I learned more about their experiences. My grandpa never brought up his time in the military, and asking always felt taboo. He only told me one story about his time in the Army. I was the only one he told anything about it to. Just from that story, however, I see why he didn't bring it up often. I felt honored by it, though, in an odd way.

In my grandpa's final moments, he didn't eat much. Even when we sat for dinner we would try to stay out in the living room and sit on the carpet while he sat on his lazy-boy chair. What he could eat was wet and soft foods and liquids. He had gone from a big bowling ball belly to a scrawny body. The food he ate either drooped from his mouth or he just couldn't hold it, but one of the food's he would still eat was tuna casserole. This is not how I want to picture my grandpa, but it is what happened. It's not the image I remember him for, but when I see tuna casserole a part of me is forced to think of him. I know the last thing he would want is for me to dwell on every detail that relates to him, or even to be sad, but that's the case. I'm sorry grandpa but I don't think I can uphold to that. I guess this is one last disagreement for the road.

A PERSONAL JOURNEY FROM WRITING TO MEDICINE: HOW WRITING SHAPED ME INTO WHO I AM, AND WHO I HOPE TO BECOME

Tessa Felker, twelfth grade

NWS Leslie Lee Nonfiction Scholarship First Place Winner

Medical textbooks, stethoscopes, and scrubs were never part of my childhood dreams. At a young age, I could be found with my nose buried in a book or a pencil pressed between my fingers, creating a callus on my ring finger that is still there today. Everyone, including myself for the longest time, felt as though I was destined to be a writer. During my teenage years, writing—specifically poetry—has helped me navigate and process my emotions more than any other medium. Writing is the core of who I am, the building block of my identity. Although I continually shared this passion for language with the people and world around me, I could not deny the gravitational pull I felt to something different.

After taking chemistry my sophomore year, I became consumed by the world of science. I was enthralled by the complex thinking it required, and how scientific approaches, ideas, and perspectives differed from any other school subject. My silent desire to pursue a medical career continued to grow throughout high school, but the fear of losing writing as a connection to myself stunted my commitment to the idea. Society has consistently taught us to view writing and science as being antithetical to each other. Doctors are stereotypically known for being detached and emotionless. This could not be further from who I am, nor does it describe the reality of medical based careers. It was not until an event in the winter of my junior year that I discovered my passion and love for personal writing could act as a future tool in becoming a physician's assistant.

It was early December, 2022, and I was standing at a podium before hundreds, throat dry, legs shaking. I had been selected to read one of my poems at an Anna Quindlen book event sponsored by the National

Writers Series, and after weeks of preparation the day had finally arrived. After reading, I received warm feedback and had the privilege of hearing how my poem resonated with others. Although this was momentous for me as a writer, my biggest takeaway from the event was something I learned from Quindlen's book, *Write For Your Life*. In the book, Quindlen dives into the importance of writing, highlighting it as a fundamental skill that allows people to make deeper connections in their day-to-day lives. However, one particular chapter of the book discusses the "Parallel Chart." Created by Dr. Rita Charon, the Parallel Chart is part of a practice called narrative medicine, in which doctors analyze their personal thoughts and emotions within a chart separate from their patient's. This was the first time I had discovered writing and science in a symbiotic relationship, and was captivated by Charon's ability to highlight the importance of the two.

When describing the need for writing, Dr. Charon states, "Unless we can attend to the interior life, the courage, if you will, of our developing doctors, we will end up with doctors who flinch when things don't go well, who abandon patients when they're dying." Where it may seem useful to foster the ability to emotionally detach, maintaining the courage to feel forges a compassionate caretaker. Writing is therapeutic, and to process the hardships of one's career, a pen could prove just as powerful as a scalpel. My ability to connect to my emotions through the vehicle of writing will benefit me when connecting with my future patients. This epiphany led me to a fortified confidence in my future goals, knowing that physician's assistant programs are continuing to integrate narrative medicine into their curricula. As I step forward into this new chapter of my life, I trust that writing will be the compass guiding me towards a future defined by empathy, healing, and boundless connection.

Contributors

2023 Art of the Story

Ryleigh Brunson is from Phoenix, Arizona. She lives in Traverse City, Michigan and is a talented drawer, actor, and writer. Her dream is to be an author. She has two cats, one dog and one Spider. She is ten years old and in the fifth grade and her birthday is June 15.

Ziva Erlenbeck is a fifth grader at TCAPS Montessori who was born in Millington, MIchigan and currently lives in Traverse City with a flock of chickens and a big backyard. Some of Ziva's hobbies are botany, biology, reading, and exploring the natural world with her great friend Eveylyn. Ziva is thankful for her teacher, Mrs. Vogel, for helping her learn and grow.

Ella (a.k.a Ellie!) Florip was born in California and currently lives in Traverse City. She's in 5th grade at Glen Lake Community Schools. Ella has three caps and loves to dance and read. *Keeper of the Last Cities* is Ella's favorite book series, by far! She wrote her first story at six years old.

Madeline Gartland lives in northern Michigan with her parents, sister, and fluffy dog, Tink! As an 8th grader she loves dancing with her dance company. When she is not busy reading or writing she loves to be out swimming in Lake Michigan. She hopes to become a good writer one day.

Madison Jancek is a 6th grader from Northern Michigan. She enjoys writing, reading, making art, and playing with her puppy Lucy. She loves the *Hunger Games* series and books by Jennifer A. Nielsen. When she grows up she wants to be a fiction Author, own her own bookstore, and make literature accessible to children in less fortunate situations.

Addison McGurn is a seventh grade in Traverse City, Michigan. When she's not reading or writing she enjoys hiking, painting and traveling with her family. Addison has one dog, one fish, and two cats she loves to snuggle with. Some of her favorite books include *The Wishing Tree, The One and Only Ivan,* and *The Marvelous Magic of Miss Mable.* Addison is excited to publish her first story and to write more with the National Writers Series.

Emma Schulert is a 5th grader at Eastern Elementary and currently resides in Old Mission Peninsula with her parents, 2 siblings, dog Violet and guinea pigs Peanut and Butterscotch. In her freetime she enjoys hanging out with friends, figure skating, reading, playing video games, baking, and writing short stories.

Sadie Snyder is a sixth grade writer from Petoskey, Michigan. She currently lives in Traverse City, Michigan, where she attends West Middle School. She loves animals, books, friends, family, and, of course, writing! If Sadie isn't writing or reading, she's writing horses at a barn. She has a lot of animals to cuddle with including a dog, cat and guinea pig. She cannot wait to write more stories!

2023 Summer Writing Fantastic Stories

Ava Montero is 13 years old and in 7th grade. In her free time she enjoys reading, writing, being outside, and spending time with family (including her dogs) and friends.

2023 Fall Antrim Raising Writers

Eden Henderson is a 5th grader in Traverse City, MI. She is on the student council. Eden loves doing crafts, art, and especially reading. Her favorite book is "Words on Fire". When Eden grows up she wants to be a teacher, a therapist, a nurse, and get a ministry degree.

Juju Pine is a seventh grader who lives in Gaylord, Michigan for the winters and camps all summer. She loves to read, write, and hug cats. Some of her favorite authors are Shannon Messenger, Jennifer Lynne Barnes, and Suzanne Collins. She can't wait for the camping season to start!

Jacob Stephens is an amateur writer who likes to play outside, and spend time with his family. He attends Bellaire middle school and hopes to be a teacher someday.

Fionnagan VandenHeuvel is a sixth-grade homeschooler that lives in Alden, Michigan with his parents and brother. He likes to telemark ski and alpine race, yo-yo, and go on nature walks with his dogs, Winnie and Birdie. He loves stories, especially realistic fiction and Garfield comics.

2023 Fall Manistee Raising Writers

Ava Deboni is a middle schooler at Manistee Area Public Schools. She loves naming trees, poetry, and stopping by the woods on a snowy evening.

Fable Wiseman is an aspiring fantasy adventurer and daydreamer. She is in the eighth grade and lives in a house full of talking cats who use a dog as security. When not taking orders from the cat majesties, she enjoys finding dark corners to read, write and draw.

Grace Condon lives with a bunch of siblings outside Manistee. Her favorite restaurant is Culver's.

Marlee Hamilton (seventh grade) lives in Manistee with her parents, dogs and siblings. This is her second time participating in the Raising Writers program in Manistee. She enjoys writing and reading.

Leah Mclellan is a freshman at Manistee High School. When she's not busy with activities and even when she's annoyed by her sister Alexis and unsatisfying novel endings, she enjoys writing short poems. This is her second time participating in Raising Writers Manistee.

Xander Lewis is a freshman in highschool. He enjoys exploring the woods and wishes he had a car so he could drive wherever he wanted.

Pandora Escartin Ortega is an exchange student in Manistee. Her home country is Spain. She loves painting in any form of expression.

Thomas Racine is a seventh grader at Manistee Middle School who really appreciates cheese. This is his second year participating in Raising Writers at the Youth Armory Project. His favorite place to visit is a small creak in Massachusetts.

2024 Winter Antrim Raising Writers

Jacob Stephens is an amateur writer who likes to play outside, and spend time with his family. He attends Bellaire middle school and hopes to be a teacher someday.

2024 Winter Manistee Raising Writers

Leah Cutler is in seventh grade at Manistee Area Public Schools. She enjoys writing and spending time with her friends.

Kate Hawkins is a 15 year old with a love for anything strange, creepy or macabre. They love Tim Burton's claymation movie corpse bride, drawing, reading, writing and going to rock concerts with their Dad. They currently reside in Northwest Michigan.

Nic Krause is a 14 year old with a passion for writing. He enjoys flying RC planes, Geocaching, and managing his vending machine business. He has a passion for the Horror genre of creative writing and poetry. His favorite color is Blue and his favorite food is Fajitas.

Thomas Racine is a seventh grader at Manistee Middle School who really appreciates cheese. This is his second year participating in Raising Writers at the Youth Armory Project. His favorite place to visit is a small creak in Massachusetts.

Marlee Hamilton (seventh grade) lives in Manistee with her parents, dogs and siblings. This is her second time participating in the Raising Writers program in Manistee. She enjoys writing and reading.

2024 Writers Create!

Annabelle Weinrich is in fourth grade of TCAPS Montessori Timberwolves in Traverse City. She has 3 cats and lives on a farm. She tries to read whenever possible when her siblings aren't bugging her. She favors cats over dogs. She shows an interest in plants and has her own cactus. She hasn't forgiven a few incidents...........

Lily Wagner is in fifth grade and homeschooled.She lives in Custer, Michigan She has one dog, one cat, three rabbits, and chickens, and ducks.She loves to read and write and if you don't catch her doing that you'll find her climbing a tree, swimming, horseback riding and much more. She has a younger brother and sister and two wonderful parents.

Marin was born in Chicago but now lives in Traverse City. Marin enjoys swimming, skateboarding, running, and writing stories! Marin is a 6th grader in middle school and is on the track team. Marin loves putting her friends into her books for fun surprises! Marin is so excited for her book to be published and hopes you enjoy reading about Hercules and his friends!

Natalie is in 4th grade and she is home schooled. She lives in Traverse City, Michigan. Her favorite book is the <u>Turtle of Oman</u> series. She has two dogs and two cats; Duke, Charlie, Joy, and Daisy. She has been a writer for about two years. Her favorite subject in school is math. Her favorite food is mac and cheese. She likes writing mystery stories and plot twists. Natalie's hobbies are writing, ballet, drawing, and flute. She is also an avid reader.

Sophia is a middle school student who enjoys writing, reading, singing, dancing, and making crafts. She also loves all kinds of animals and wants to be a vet some day. Sophia has a pet cat who inspires many of her stories. She began writing books when she was five years old and has continued to write on various topics ever since.

Soren is a fourth grader at Eastern Elementary School. He lives in Traverse City. Soren loves Math, Science,and playing on the playground. Outside of school he likes to play with his toys, especially his Mega Cyborg Hand. His favorite book is titled, <u>Investigators.</u> He has been busy writing for eight years.

Ziva Erlenbeck is a fifth grader at TCAPS Montessori who was born in Millington, MIchigan and currently lives in Traverse City with a flock of chickens and a big backyard. Some of Ziva's hobbies are botany, biology, reading, and exploring the natural world with her great friend Eveylyn. Ziva is thankful for her teacher, Mrs. Vogel, for helping her learn and grow.

Writers Studio

Hunter Arnold is a junior at Kingsley High School and a member of the Career Tech Writers Studio. For twelve years she has been part of the Northwest Michigan Fair showing swine and rabbits. She has a deep interest in writing and plans to major in creative writing.

Minnie Bardenhagen is a high school senior from Suttons Bay and a member of the Career Tech Writers Studio. She participates in theater, choir, band, and softball. Her passion is music and plans to go to Northwestern Michigan College.

Kaihe Brown is a junior at Elk Rapids High School and Career Tech Writers Studio who is a self proclaimed "loud and proud weirdo." He plans on taking a career in voice acting and making comics. "I'm pretty much always my target audience."

Evelyn Choate is a junior at Traverse City Central High School as well as Career Tech. She can play three instruments and prefers the electric guitar.

Reegan Craker is a senior at Suttons Bay High School and a second year at Career Tech Writers Studio program. She enjoys reading and illustrating and plans on majoring in digital cinema at Northern Michigan University.

James Eady is a junior at Kalkaska High School attending Writers Studio at Career Tech. He likes playing in band and can play the mellophone, trumpet and clarinet. He wants to pursue a career as a band director and plans to run for the position of drum major/minor.

Elaina Farmer is a junior at Mancelona High School and Career Tech Writers Studio. They plan on making a career out of the content they create, both in writing and videos. They are also passionate about their art and dance. They are part of their school's band and volunteer in the school-run store.

Tatum Alice Fineout is a junior from Traverse Senior West Senior High School and is a student in the Career Tech Writers Studio program. She enjoys writing, reading, and mathematics. She's considered many career fields and now plans to attend college after highschool to become an advanced mathematics teacher.

Lillian Greenman is a junior from Traverse City Central High School and attends Career Tech's Writers Studio program as a first-year student. She enjoys cheerleading, painting, and hikes with her husky, Jewel. After highschool she plans to explore her options in trade schooling.

Brent Mankowski is a junior from North Central Academy and Career Tech Writers Studio. He aims to be able to write his own stories in his own mindset, as well as to explore the world of art and the world in general.

Randale McCuien is a senior at Traverse City Central High School and attends Career Tech Writers Studio as a second-year student. He is a violinist, track and field athlete and choral musician. He plans to attend college on an athletic scholarship, and will major in theater arts.

Lucas McSwain is a senior from Traverse City Central High School and Northwest Ed Career Tech's Writers Studio. He aspires to travel and write about the world to meet new people and explore new places. He enlisted in the United States Navy as a Cyber Warfare Technician to start his travel and career.

Dominic Montoya-Arlt, age 18, has lived in northwestern Michigan his entire life and doesn't plan on changing that fact anytime soon. He is eager to pursue a bone-chilling career as a librarian and will fill up his spare time with writing, tabletop games, and vomiting out words in a vague approximation of singing.

Mason Moran is a senior at Traverse City Central High School and attends Career Tech's Writers Studio as a second-year student. He enjoys writing poetry, singing, playing ukulele, and acting. He will be attending Northwestern Michigan College next year, and is planning on studying music.

Ella Mullens is a junior at Bellaire High School and Career Tech Writers Studio. She is a creative writer and musician who is passionate about inspiring others through art. She plans on attending Northwestern Michigan College after high school.

Isabelle Plamondon is a junior at Suttons Bay High School and a first year at Career Tech Writers Studio. She enjoys drama, writing, and raising animals. After high school, she hopes to study forensic behavioral sciences and make a difference in the world.

Vincent Redman is a senior at Traverse City Central High School and Career Tech Writers Studio. As an adult he plans to go to medical school and one day become a psychiatrist.

Madeline Rowney is a high school senior from Traverse City Central High School and Career Tech Writers Studio. She holds a deep passion for writing, and is attending Goldsmiths, University of London for journalism in the fall.

Lola Russell is a junior at The Greenspire High School and Career Tech Writers Studio. She is passionate about learning and nature, and hopes to inspire people through creative writing in the future.

Isabel Schmidt is a senior at Suttons Bay High School and Career Tech Writers Studio. She enjoys writing and reading, and is hoping to attend Grand Valley State University for writing in the fall. Isabel hopes she can inspire young readers and writers with her work.

Alicia Streeter is a senior at Traverse Central High School and Career Tech Writers Studio. They enjoy creative activities like drawing and DND. In the future, they hope to become a paleontologist.

Chloe Taylor is a junior at Mancelona High School and Career Tech Writers Studio. She enjoys writing fiction, painting, and playing the tenor saxophone. After high school, she hopes to inspire people with her stories.

2024 Literary Short Story

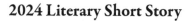

Kamea Helmstetter (known by most as Kat) is a junior at her online school, Fusion Global Academy. During her free time, she is most often found at her taekwondo academy or writing.

Anabelle Joya is a 10th grade writer, poet, and student. She likes to read, write, and watch anime. She attends Churchland High and lives with her family in Virginia.

Tess Tarchak-Hiss is a sophomore at Traverse City West Senior High, originally from the lovely land of New Jersey, and she's been writing since she was catapulted from the womb. She enjoys playing roller derby with her friends, passenger princessing, making rough-looking imovies, spraypainting, and depending on who's asking, long walks on the beach.

Laura Busick lives in Bellaire Mi with her parents and two brothers. She and her brothers are homeschooled by her mom. Laura likes to read, play soccer, jog, do crafts, sew, do various outdoor activities, and help her parents.

2024 Scholarship Winners

Emma Newman-Bale is graduating this year, 2024, from Traverse City Central High School. Beginning in the fall, she will be attending Michigan State University and will pursue a major of Graphic or Interior Design and minor in Japanese. She lives with her family in Traverse City.

Kaitlyn Andrews is an upcoming high school graduate who loves writing, art, and anything remotely musical. Kaitlyn is pursuing a bachelor's degree in elementary education with the upmost desire of becoming a nurturing and positive influence on the youth of society. She plans to attend the University of Mary in the fall, where she is excited to open a new chapter of her life with the high hopes of surviving her first North Dakota winter.

Kailyn Groves is a junior at Traverse City Central High School, where she is a staff writer for the Black and Gold Quarterly. This is her first year in journalism and as a BGQ staff writer. Apart from journalism, she writes for creative writing.

Kendra Couturier is a senior at Lake Leelanau St. Mary. She enjoys tending her garden, running, and various creative pursuits. She also finds joy in stringing together snippets of moments in nature to create poetry.

Lola Russell is a junior at The Greenspire High School and Career Tech Writers Studio. She is passionate about learning and nature, and hopes to inspire people through creative writing in the future.

Lucas McSwain is a senior from Traverse City Central High School and Northwest Ed Career Tech's Writers Studio. He aspires to travel and write about the world to meet new people and explore new places. He enlisted in the United States Navy as a Cyber Warfare Technician to start his travel and career.

Tessa Felker is a graduating senior at Elk Rapids High School. She is attending the University of Michigan in the fall, and plans to major in biology with a minor in creative writing on a pre-PA track.

Photography

The middle son of three boys, Jonas Carlson is in seventh grade at Manistee Middle High School. He plays trombone in band and enjoys urban exploring. He has an interest in buildings and landscape photography.

Acknowledgments

The pieces you find in this volume were written by students in the NWS Raising Writers youth programs and the North Ed Writers Studio. These programs are composed of students who are passionate about writing!

Raising Writers is literally made possible by the time and generosity of countless people, including our many volunteers, our kind community, and our generous donors, sponsors, and grantors: the Michigan Arts and Culture Council, the National Endowment for the Arts, the Gerstacker Foundation, and the Dragonfly Fund.

Putting together the *National Writers Series Traverse City Literary Journal* was a team effort, led by Ari Mokdad, the NWS education director who super-charged our Raising Writers program this past year and worked endless hours putting together this wonderful journal.

Thanks also go to Mission Point Press and Andrea Reider for the book design. We are hugely grateful for our NWS instructors Kelly Almer, Lauren K. Carlson, Kevin Fitton, Karin Killian, and David Hornibrook, along with Writers Studio instructor Teresa Scollon. They provided wonderful instruction and valuable feedback to students on every single piece you'll read here.

We also included the winning pieces of our NWS scholarship winners. Thank you to Gina Thornbury and the Grand Traverse Regional Community Foundation for their partnership in running the scholarship program—and to the judges who made the hard decisions of selecting the eight finalists and semi-finalists from dozens of submissions.

Finally, hats off to Shirley and Chip Hoagland for sponsoring the book launch of the *Literary Journal* at the Alluvion, where students will read their work in front of supportive friends of family!

Our biggest thanks are given to the many young writers who worked so hard on their entries and had the courage to share their words with the public.

Thank you to all!

Anne Stanton
NWS Executive Director and the NWS Board of Trustees

Made in the USA
Middletown, DE
05 May 2024

53848887R00175